I0213200

THE
MASSAPEQUAS

TWO THOUSAND YEARS OF HISTORY

THE
MASSAPEQUAS

TWO THOUSAND YEARS OF HISTORY

GEORGE KIRCHMANN

The
History
PRESS

Published by The History Press
Charleston, SC
www.historypress.com

Copyright © 2021 by George Kirchmann
All rights reserved

First published 2021

ISBN 9781540248015

Library of Congress Control Number: 2021934113

Notice: The information in this book is true and complete to the best of our knowledge. It is offered without guarantee on the part of the author or The History Press. The author and The History Press disclaim all liability in connection with the use of this book.

All rights reserved. No part of this book may be reproduced or transmitted in any form whatsoever without prior written permission from the publisher except in the case of brief quotations embodied in critical articles and reviews.

CONTENTS

ACKNOWLEDGEMENTS

No history can be written without the participation of many people who provide valuable assistance throughout the process. I am indebted first of all to the Historical Society of the Massapequas. I have been a trustee for twenty years and have connected with so many other trustees who have facilitated this project in many ways. I am especially grateful to Bill Colfer, past president, who has presented countless lectures and discussions of Massapequa's history. He served as the administrator for the Village of Massapequa Park and was a longtime member of the Massapequa Fire Department. During those years, he acquired an encyclopedic knowledge of the area's history. Charles Mackie, current president, has been continually supportive of my efforts and opened the doors to information contained in the historical society's files. Jeanne Burns read several sections of this book and offered incisive comments. Lovey Bryson, whose family traces their origins to the Massapequas in the 1870s, was significantly helpful for the early years of the twentieth century. Above all, Arlene Goodenough, past president of the historical society, was very generous in sharing her insights on the organization's beginnings and early development, as well as the history of Old Grace Church.

Don Nobile, a longtime teacher and administrator in Massapequa's School District 23, was especially helpful for the development of the school system after 1945 and the role of the Massapequa Teachers' Union. Charles Sulc, former superintendent, shared his knowledge of the school system in the '80s, especially during the tenure of Superintendent Herbert Pluschau.

ACKNOWLEDGEMENTS

Anne Marie Bellizi made school district publications available to me and answered questions on several small but significant topics.

Connie Belagrinos provided access to the Water District's history, and Linda Tuminello found Massapequa Park's files for me, especially regarding Fitzmaurice Flying Field and the Long Island Rail Road. The late Eugene Bryson familiarized me with the Delancey Floyd-Jones Free Library and directed me to its historical documents.

The Long Island Studies Institute at Hofstra University houses an impressive collection of Long Island historical information. The staff made available to me the Jones family files, as well as historical journals containing articles about many topics related to the Massapequas.

I am grateful to The History Press for accepting my manuscript for publication. J. Banks Smither provided valuable guidance through the entire process. Ryan Finn read the text carefully and made many helpful suggestions as well as corrections. Maddison Potter guided me through the company's sales and marketing activities.

My children—Adam, Elizabeth, Andrea and Matthew—encouraged my efforts, and my wife, Valerie, supported me throughout the writing process, reading my drafts, listening to my sometimes endless explanations and encouraging me to keep moving the creative process forward. To her above all I offer my love and thanks.

This book was written to appeal to two audiences: those who know quite a bit about Massapequa's history and those who are minimally or not at all familiar with it. I've used primary and secondary sources and have provided notes throughout, but I've attempted to preserve an informal tone, with reference to so many personalities that shaped Massapequa's history and with examples that compare past to present conditions.

Please note that any errors or omissions are entirely my responsibility.

INTRODUCTION

The first issue that should be resolved is the title of this book. *The Massapequas*, rather than *Massapequa*, is the appropriate title because there are four areas that will be described. East Massapequa is the area east of Carman's Road from the Southern State Parkway to South Oyster Bay. It had its own zip code for many years, and children who live there attend the Amityville schools. North Massapequa is the area north of the Southern State Parkway up to Boundary Avenue, east of Route 135 and west of the Bethpage Parkway. It has its own fire department. The Incorporated Village of Massapequa Park is in the geographic middle of the Massapequas. It was created in 1931 and has its own mayor, trustees and governmental services. The rest of the area is known as Massapequa and is referred to as a hamlet—that is, a small settlement, generally smaller than a village, without a separate governing body. All four entities are part of the town of Oyster Bay and encompass the area from Boundary Avenue/Southern State Parkway on the north, the Nassau-Suffolk County border on the east, the Tackapausha Preserve to the west and South Oyster Bay on the south. It is located in the southeastern portion of Nassau County, separated by South Oyster Bay from Jones Beach.

This hodgepodge of locales contains thousands of residents in a suburban setting that varies little throughout the area. Most residents live in one-family private houses, although rental units are allowed in areas other than Massapequa Park. Many residents take the Long Island Railroad to work in New York City, while others work locally. Most children attend the public Massapequa school system (seven thousand students), although some attend St. Rose of Lima Catholic School. Businesses are grouped along Broadway and Hicksville Road, from Merrick Road up to the Southern State Parkway, along Merrick Road and Sunrise Highway and on Park Boulevard in the Village of Massapequa Park.

Massapequa, separate from Massapequa Park, contains fifty thousand inhabitants. The total population of the area, including Massapequa Park, is about seventy thousand. This book will show how the area became what it is today, from unusual beginnings with a sparse population centered on one family for many decades to explosive growth after World War II.

Chapter 1

BEGINNINGS

Native Americans lived on Long Island for several thousand years before white encroachment. We know about their presence in the Massapequas from a cache of tools uncovered when Massapequa Lake was drained in September 1969 to combat bacteria in the water that was polluting Alhambra Beach downstream. The collection was uncovered by workers who were installing a drainage pipe. They notified Nassau County's Garvies Point Museum in Glen Cove. Analysts removed most of the collection, numbering 184 blades, and they are now on display in the museum. The Massapequa Historical Society also has several dozen, which were collected by a local resident and donated. They are similar to caches uncovered in Mattituck and Peconic on the North Fork.

Most of the tools were made of yellow jasper, which is not found along the East Coast. They bear a striking similarity to artifacts identified with the Adena culture, which flourished in Ohio until about 100 BCE, when its members were forced east by the Hopewell culture. Historians believe they were brought here for trade or barter with local residents and hidden for later retrieval. Each artifact is about three and a half inches long and one and five-eighths inches wide, with sharp points that were chipped in. They were arranged in rows horizontally one to two feet below the ground. Whoever buried them may have left them closer to the surface, but they were likely covered when Massapequa Lake was dug out in 1837. They were buried sometime between 75 BCE and 400 CE and represent the only physical evidence we have of Native American settlement during the Woodland period, between 1000 BCE and 1600 CE.

Native American tools found in 1969. *Courtesy of Garvies Point Museum, Nassau County, New York.*

The tribe that lived in this area was variously known as Marsapeags, Mashpeags or Massapeags because of the location. The term translates as "Place of Many Waters" or "Great Water Land" because of the many brooks, streams and rivers that run down from the hilly center of Long Island. Natives had access to abundant supplies of fish and local game and grew vegetables north of the bay, near the present-day Southern State Parkway. The term *Massapequa* came into common usage in the 1890s.

Historians estimate that there were about six thousand Native Americans living on Long Island when whites began to settle the area in the early 1600s. The Massapequa area became a gathering place because its distance offered protection from tribes that regularly raided from Connecticut, taking goods, women and crops and frightening the relatively peaceful Long Island natives. There were attempts to categorize the Native Americans into tribes—thirteen, according to historian Paul Bailey—but that division tends to blur the complex relations among tribal groups, which were really extended families whose members often intermarried and who moved around the island to find better grazing lands. The Massapequas (or Marshpeagues or some other variant) lived peaceably in the area for many generations.

Native American men wore moccasins and loincloths and often wore deerskin or leather in cold weather. They hunted with arrows and fished with rudimentary fishing poles. Women wore leggings that came up to their knees and a robe. They farmed the land and tended to move to nearby areas when the land became unfertile. They shared their crops with other extended families and engaged in very few squabbles. They were thus extremely vulnerable to English and Dutch invaders, who were determined to settle throughout Long Island and possessed the weapons and military training to overcome the natives' resistance.[1]

Judge Samuel Jones in 1821 spoke of a massacre of natives organized and directed in 1643 by Colonel John Underhill, who was directed by the Dutch governor of New York, Peter Stuyvesant, to subdue them so the area could be settled. There are many examples of skirmishes between the natives and the Dutch (and later the English) on Long Island, but evidence suggests that the attack by Underhill's forces occurred farther west, in Maspeth, which was at that time experiencing repeated clashes between the local native tribes and the Dutch settlers. The latter were eager to control the area, which was close to New Amsterdam. The Dutch had employed Underhill in several skirmishes in the

Native American wigwam. *Courtesy of Garvies Point Museum, Nassau County, New York.*

13

western part of Long Island in the 1640s. Their relations with natives farther east were more amicable, centering on trade and land exchanges. They were concerned with the growing presence of the English and were determined to maintain good relations with the local native groups.

Native settlers built a walled fort near South Oyster Bay. It was originally considered by historians as a site for protection, but extensive recent studies indicate that it was likely built by native tribes under direction of the Dutch around 1655 as a trading post and gathering place. The fort was surrounded by stakes about twelve feet high. Its remnants were discovered by Ralph Solecki, a young archaeologist who followed up on tales of such a fortification written down by white settlers. He excavated the site in 1938, and the Town of Oyster Bay declared it a historic site and erected a marker on the property. The vague outline of a fort can still be seen today at the site near Gloucester Road and Sunset Boulevard at the northwest corner of Sunset playground.

The Native American population fell drastically throughout the 1600s, the result of diseases brought by Europeans, attacks by Dutch and English forces and the gradual withdrawal from an area that had become increasingly inhospitable. A smallpox epidemic from 1659 to 1664 wiped out many extended families and left the remaining settlers helpless against the increasing numbers of Dutch and English settlers. Jasper Daenkaerts wrote in 1679 that "there is now not 1/10th part of the Indians that there once were…and that now there are 20 or 30 times as many [white settlers]." Native peoples either moved onto reservations (Poospatuck and Montaukett in eastern Long Island), moved west to unsettled areas or assimilated into the general population. Many became trackers and whalers, sailing out of many sites on both the north shore and south shore. The estimated population of six thousand Native Americans in 1600 was whittled down to fewer than one thousand by 1700. The white population was eight thousand and growing.

Sag Harbor and Cold Spring Harbor became known as whaling centers in the mid-1700s, but whaling was a common activity throughout Long Island, starting in the 1650s. One of the earlier whaling sites was actually located where the East Bathhouse of Jones Beach stands today. It was begun in 1705 by Thomas Jones, who employed Native Americans and Black slaves to hunt, kill and process whales, which were prized then for their blubber and oil. The location was ideal because whales were readily available a short distance from the shore and what is today Jones Beach was a series of smaller beaches that were reshaped by the ocean, and that provided ideal locations for processing whales.

Native American whalers. *Author's collection.*

Whalers used small dugout canoes built by Native Americans that were maneuverable and very buoyant. They usually carried six men: one steerer at the back, four rowers and one harpooner at the front. Earlier whalers used stone and wood harpoons, but later hunters, provisioned by white entrepreneurs, used metal spears, an example of the intrusion of modern weaponry on an ancient practice.[2]

TACKAPAUSHA

Tackapausha was sachem of the several tribes that loosely gathered in the Massapequa area. He signed several treaties with the English, who had forced the Dutch off western Long Island in 1664, and gradually ceded control of the entire area by the time of his death, which was estimated to be 1697. He counseled other tribal leaders that resistance to the Dutch and later the English was futile, and he was able to secure treaties that provided restricted living areas for native tribes as well as material goods that today seem insignificant to us (pots, coats, knives). The history of relations between Long Island natives and white settlers is one of violent conquest of overmatched peaceful natives who were steadily forced off lands where they had resided for centuries.[3]

A 1639 treaty between the Dutch West India Company and native tribes gave the Dutch all that is today eastern Brooklyn and Queens and Nassau County. Seaford was settled in 1643 and Amityville in 1658, but there were no white settlements in the Massapequas until many years later, in large part because of the landownership activities that transpired in the second half of the seventeenth century. These were centered on the influential Townsend family, who had settled in Oyster Bay, far to the north of the Massapequas.

Several disparate groups of English settlers from Connecticut and Rhode Island had settled in the Oyster Bay area and signed treaties with the native tribes in the 1650s. Peter Stuyvesant, who nominally controlled the area, was powerless to resist the steady English encroachments because of the growing complexity of New Amsterdam and challenges from wealthy merchants who resented his efforts to control their activities. Several treaties were signed and agreements made, involving Natives, English and Dutch, resulting in the helter-skelter settlement of the area on Long Island Sound first known as the Town Spot.

The Anglican Church was England's official church, but there were dissenters, called Puritans, who disliked the lack of discipline within the church. Others who grew in the 1640s and became even more vexing to the

Council Rock. *Author's collection.*

British were the Quakers, who resisted formal religious services, especially those that mimicked the Roman Catholic rite. Several English subjects became Quakers, including the Townsend family, although there is some dispute whether they actually joined the movement. They were clearly sympathetic to it, as were many other Oyster Bay settlers.

George Fox became a leader of the Quaker movement and preached throughout central Long Island in the mid-1600s. His best known preaching site was Council Rock, located just west of the township of Oyster Bay. He stood on the rock and preached sermons that attracted many converts. The Dutch and later the British were uncomfortable with his preaching but refrained from banishing him because of his popularity. There is a marker in front of the rock on Lake Avenue, one hundred yards south of West Main Street.

THE TOWNSEND FAMILY

Three brothers—John, Henry and Richard Townsend—had come from England in the 1620s, settling first in Rhode Island and then in Jamaica and Flushing. They were involved in writing the Flushing Remonstrance of 1657, the first document in the New World to insist on freedom of religion and clear separation of church and state. It was aimed at Dutch governor Peter Stuyvesant and was designed to allow the newly formed Quakers to practice their religious beliefs freely. The Townsends were nominally Episcopalians but were partial to Quaker beliefs. This document became the basis of the First Amendment to the Constitution, forbidding any establishment of a national church or of an official religion. The Remonstrance stated:

> *The law of love, peace and liberty in the states extending to Jews, Turks, and Egyptians, as they are considered sons of Adam, which is the glory of the outward state of Holland, soe love, peace and liberty, extending to all in Christ Jesus, condemns hatred, war and bondage....* [O]*ur desire is not to offend one of his little ones, in whatsoever form, name or title he appears in, whether Presbyterian, Independent, Baptist, or Quaker, but shall be glad to see anything but God in any of them...which is the true law both of Church and State; for our Savior sayeth this is the law and the prophets.*[4]

The Remonstrance was written by Edward Hart, Cleric, and signed by thirty residents, among them John and Henry Townsend.

The Townsends were forced out of Flushing because of their religious views and settled in Oyster Bay around 1653, where they were welcomed because of their industriousness and willingness to take on a variety of tasks. About one hundred white settlers lived in Oyster Bay at the time, most of them English. The young settlement needed structure, and the Townsends provided it, holding a variety of offices and mediating in disputes among the property owners who had settled there. Several Townsends were surveyors, which was considered the most important public office at the time because of the disputes over territory with the natives and among the new settlers.[5]

Henry Townsend was one of the signatories of the 1658 treaty that gave several other Oyster Bay leaders and him ownership of the land that became Massapequa. They signed it with Sachem Tackapausha and other sachems of the Rockaway and Secatogue tribes, providing kettles, guns, powder and shot, cloth, swords, shoes, stockings and strong waters in exchange for rights to use the land and will it to their descendants. They also gained the right to erect "a free highway...for horse and cart" (Kings Highway, later South Country Road, eventually Merrick Road). In 1704, the British governor directed that a road four rods wide (a rod equals 16.5 feet) be built from Brooklyn to Southampton. When completed, it was named the Kings Highway and was for many years the main thoroughfare between New York and Montauk. Henry Townsend and the other signatories eventually sold the entire parcel to Thomas Townsend.

Some native leaders may not have grasped the implications of contemporary developments, but Tackapausha understood that native people were losing control of land where they had lived for centuries. Tackapausha's position was weakened further by the smallpox epidemic (1659–64), which ravaged entire communities. The English and Dutch provided little assistance, preferring to isolate themselves from native tribes so they did not contract or spread the disease. There are no records of the number of deaths, but it was clearly substantial, with reports of entire extended families dying within days of contracting it. After this experience, Tackapausha and other sachems were forced to adapt new strategies, including merger with other native communities, intermarriage with African Americans and relocation.[6]

John Townsend died in 1668, and his widow, Elizabeth, divided up his property among her five children. She gave the large portion of land to the south of Oyster Bay to her eldest son, Thomas, who held various positions in the town, such as constable, surveyor, recorder and justice. Thomas was respected by all who knew him, especially the Native American chiefs, with whom he negotiated for land. In 1679, he signed a treaty with Tackapausha, chief of the Massapequas, that gave him just about all the land between Seaford and Amityville and from Hardscrabble (later Farmingdale) to the ocean. The total size was six thousand acres.

Chapter 2

THOMAS JONES
MAKES HIS MARK

Thomas Jones, the first European settler in the Massapequas, appeared on the North American scene in 1692, bringing with him a splendidly varied set of life experiences. He was born in Strabane, Northern Ireland, about 1665 and was a member of the Episcopal Church, yet he fought on the side of Catholic King James II at the Battle of the Boyne in 1688 (the losing side of what is known as the Glorious Revolution). This experience earned him the title "Major," which was commonly used to identify him during his life and among his descendants. After King James's defeat, he and his troops accepted exile to France. Jones ended up in Jamaica, witnessing the great earthquake there in 1692. He was involved as a pirate (although his descendants insisted that he was really a privateer), was captured and tried in a New York Court, with six others, and was the only one set free because he produced his Letter of Marque from the exiled King James, which was accepted by the court. He then moved to Rhode Island, where he met Thomas Townsend, who had moved to Portsmouth as its sheriff.[7]

Thomas Townsend had five children, among them a daughter, Freelove, born in 1674. She met and fell in love with Thomas Jones, who had become friendly with her father. They married and settled in Oyster Bay, in a house Thomas Townsend had built for himself but gave to his daughter and son-in-law. The house was remarkable for its foot-thick walls and gun slots on the upper floors, providing protection from whomever might be a threat. The house was attacked several times during the American Revolution and bore a number of bullet holes in its walls. It was torn down in 1922.

The Massapequas became one of the last communities to be settled on Long Island. The Astoria-Maspeth area was the first, in 1636, and others close to the Massapequas were settled soon after: Seaford in 1643, Oyster Bay and Huntington in 1653 and Amityville in 1658. Why was this area settled so late? An insight can be gained from an exchange between Thomas Townsend and his son John. Thomas had originally offered the land to John in 1692, but he had declined, asking, "Does my father want me to go out of the world?" The area was sparsely occupied, filled with streams, swamps and rivers and bordered by interconnected sandy islands that blocked the Atlantic Ocean. There were no roads leading down directly from Oyster Bay, so traveling would be difficult. In 1696, Thomas Townsend offered son-in-law Thomas Jones his large tract of land along Long Island's south shore. Thomas Jones saw it as an opportunity to develop his own source of power and wealth. He willingly accepted his father-in-law's offer on June 29, 1696, and moved there with his wife, Freelove, settling on a parcel that totaled six thousand acres.

Thomas and Freelove Jones suffered the loss of their first child, Sarah, in August 1696. It is likely they were not living at Fort Neck because of the time it would have taken Thomas to build his brick house. We know that Sarah is buried at the Clifton Burying Ground in Newport, Rhode Island. They may have lived there or nearby because Thomas Townsend was sheriff of Portsmouth, Rhode Island, at the time. Freelove likely felt more comfortable giving birth in a settled area with family and friends nearby. The baby's burial was one of the first at a very old Newport Cemetery. The site can be identified from burial records, but there is no marker or headstone.

Freelove and Thomas settled in a house that was unusual not only because it was the only one in the Massapequas but also because it was made of red brick. Thomas may have used his father-in-law's house in Oyster Bay as a model, realizing that he might still need protection from the Native Americans who lingered in the area. There is no record that he or his family were ever attacked or threatened in any way, either by Native Americans or by other settlers in nearby Seaford or Amityville. The house may have been built just east of the Massapequa River, although a 1797 map places it north of today's Merrick Road, near a stream that was expanded to create Massapequa Lake in 1837.

Thomas Jones held several important posts in Queens County. He was, at various times, Episcopal church warden, elected by Oyster Bay church leaders (1703); high sheriff (1704); major of the Queens County Militia (1706); justice of the peace (1710); ranger general (1710); and

Queens County supervisor. All these posts brought money, notoriety and power, which he exercised in such a way that he was esteemed by many contemporaries. The ranger general title gave him the monopoly on whaling and other fisheries on Long Island's north and south shores. Under a 1705 license from Governor Cornbury, Jones established a whaling station on the beach that was close to the Jones Beach East Bathhouse today and employed Native Americans and Black slaves in the capture and processing of whales. The enterprise proved very lucrative and was continued by Native Americans after Jones's death in 1713.[8]

His most interesting experience may have been one that occurred about 1709, when Governor Cornbury sent two armed emissaries from New York to arrest Jones for nonpayment of fees, probably related to whaling, which Cornbury wanted to control. Jones ordered his servants to set out a lavish feast and invited the emissaries to sit with him and discuss their grievances. He then said they could either have lunch with him or fight with pistols, two of which he carried. They agreed to have lunch and returned to Lord Cornbury with Thomas's request that he visit him. Cornbury did, and the two got along very well from that time.

Freelove and Thomas Jones headstones. *Author's collection.*

Jones made several land purchases during his time in Fort Neck from Native Americans and from English settlers. His property stretched from the ocean to Manetto Hill and eventually to Cold Spring Harbor. In his will, he named Freelove executor and divided his land among his three sons—David, William and Thomas—with the provision that enough land be sold to provide for their education. David at fourteen was the oldest of Thomas's children at his death in 1713, so they would need to be cared for by Freelove until they reached maturity. A genealogy chart detailing Jones's family was given to the Delancey Floyd-Jones Free Library in 1970 and is available for review.

Upon Jones's death, his wife, Freelove, returned to Oyster Bay with her children, doubtless for her safety as well as her family's. She married an Irish captain, Timothy Bagley, in 1716 and remained in Oyster Bay until her death in 1726. She managed the family's extensive property and bought additional parcels in the Oyster Bay area. She was buried next to Thomas on the bank of the Massapequa River and was joined there later by her son David and his wife, Anna. Their remains were exhumed in 1892 because of the rising water level and were reinterred at the Floyd-Jones Cemetery, which is located at the back part of Massapequa's historic complex on Merrick Road.

Thomas Jones's headstone reads:

> *Here Lyes Interd the Body of Major Thomas Jones, Who Came from Straubane, in the Kingdom of Ireland, Settled Here and Died December 1713. From Distant Lands to This Wild Waste He Came, This Seat He Chose and There He Fixd His Name, Long May His Sons This Peaceful Spot Injoy, and No Ill Fate His Offspring Here Annoy.*

Freelove, who is buried next to him, has this on her headstone:

> *Here Lyes Interd the Body of Freelove Bagley Daughter of Captn Thomas Townsend of Rhode Island. First Married to Maj Thomas Jones. After His Death to Major Timothy Bagley. She Died July 1726.*[9]

Thomas's Old Brick House became the source of many legends. It was written that a black crow hovered over him at his death and then flew out the bedroom window, which could never be closed again. The front door had to be replaced on several occasions because it flew open and broke without explanation. People passing by in the evening saw lights in the building, which was supposedly unoccupied. Many nearby residents considered the building haunted and steered clear of it at night. These stories simply serve to enhance Thomas Jones's reputation as an unusual and unique settler. When the Old Brick House was destroyed in 1837, at the time Massapequa Manor was built, David Floyd-Jones wrote about its heritage in his poem "On the Destruction of the Brick House in Massapequa":

> *His sons for many generations here*
> *Have lived nor ever felt misfortunes tide*
> *Dash its stern against them—sorrow's tear*
> *Hath seldom dimmed their eye—aged they did*
> *Within their walls no longer shall their children dwell*
> *Thou hallowed pile; loved een in ruins, fare thee well.*[10]

Chapter 3

JONES DESCENDANTS

W illiam Jones, born in 1708, was the first of Thomas's descendants to settle in the area. He built a house to the west of the Old Brick House, large enough to accommodate his fifteen children, eleven of whom survived to adulthood. He eventually had ninety-five grandchildren. He purchased additional land in the Fort Neck area and used it to raise cattle and provide grass for neighboring farmers. He died in 1779 and was buried at a newly established cemetery south of his house that is today called the West Neck Cemetery (also known as the Jones Cemetery) and sits on the south side of Merrick Road. It appears that his house was in the vicinity of today's Fairfield School.[11]

Thomas Jr., born in 1702, established a ferry service from Matinecock, west of Oyster Bay, to Connecticut. It was powered by horses walking on a movable platform and proved to be very popular because there were no bridges across Long Island Sound or even over the various rivers that ran down to the Sound. Sadly, "The ferryboat of Maj. Thomas Jones, of Oyster Bay, was overset in the Sound, and himself, his negro, three men and one woman who were passengers, with six horses, were all drowned on Nov. 13, 1741."[12]

Thomas Jr. had at least one Black slave, according to this quote. His brother David also owned slaves, as documented in his 1768 will. He identified nine slaves and specified which of his children would inherit them upon his death. David Richard, his grandson, was bequeathed a slave. He later became David Richard Floyd-Jones, the first to carry that family name.

In 1799, New York State abolished slavery, with the exceptions that current slaves could remain bound until 1828 and slaves born after 1799 would be indentured servants until 1828. There is no record that the Jones or Floyd-Jones families released their slaves before 1828.

Thomas Jones made no mention in his will of slaves, but it seems likely that he owned several, using them in his whaling activities. Black slaves and Native Americans constituted the vast majority of crews involved in whaling activities throughout Long Island.[13]

Thomas's son David had a distinguished legal career. He was a Queens County judge, a member of the New York Assembly from 1737 until 1758, Speaker of the Assembly for several of these years and then judge of the New York Supreme Court. One of his most important acts was fostering and approving creation of the College of the City of New York, later renamed Columbia University. He was also the owner of his father's land because of the entail laws of the time, which automatically vested property to the eldest son. He lived in New York City until 1773, when he completed a large estate that he named Tryon Hall, in honor of the governor at the time.

Tryon Hall was one of the very few houses standing in the Massapequas before the American Revolution. In addition to the Red Brick House and William Jones's house, there was a small cottage in East Massapequa, probably built by the Carman family, who had settled in Amityville and built a mill near Merrick Road. The house dates from 1765 and is included in Oyster Bay's List of Historic Structures, but proof of its exact date is sparse. There is also another house, on Merrick Road near Massapequa Lake, that was apparently built in the 1760s, but documentation there is shaky also. It is clear that there was very little settlement of the Massapequas before 1800, in contrast to nearby Seaford, Amityville and Oyster Bay.

David Jones built Tryon Hall in order to attract his son Thomas to settle in a less contentious area. Thomas had graduated from Yale and practiced law in New York City, becoming corporation counsel and later succeeding his father as Supreme Court justice. He held strong beliefs in favor of English rule and earned a reputation as a steadfast supporter of the Crown's authority over its New York subjects. For this he was often involved in contentious discussions with other public figures. After the Battle of Lexington, he proposed, at a meeting of several judges summoned by Governor Tryon, "that the military should be called out and the riot act read, and if the mob did not thereupon disperse, to apprehend and imprison the ringleaders."[14]

Tryon Hall. *Courtesy of the Historical Society of the Massapequas.*

When the American Revolution broke out, Judge Thomas Jones became the target of criticism from Patriots. He was labeled a Tory and bore the title proudly. He was arrested twice in 1776 by the Provincial Congress and released on promise of not providing information about the Continental army to British forces. In 1779, he was kidnapped by Patriot troops, who broke into Tryon Hall during a party and took him to Connecticut, where he was kept at the home of General Gold Silliman, a Patriot who had been captured by the British and brought to Long Island. Silliman's wife attended to wounds Jones had received during his capture. After staying there for several months, he was exchanged for Governor Silliman literally in the middle of Long Island Sound, as the two sides transferred the men from one boat to the other. Jones and Silliman had a cordial meal during the exchange, as both had attended Yale and had become friends in the 1750s.

In 1779, the New York legislature identified fifty-two citizens as enemies of the Revolution because of their activities or positions in the Tory government. Jones was one of them, as a state Supreme Court judge and an enthusiastic supporter of the Crown. For this reason, he and other "enemies" were named in an Act of Attainder and were ordered to leave the American colonies, as well as forfeit all their possessions, without benefit of trial or due process. Those who remained were subject to being shot on sight. The bill is titled "An Act for the Forfeiture and Sale of the Estates of

Above: Anne and Judge Thomas Jones.
Courtesy of the Historical Society of the Massapequas.

Right: David Richard Floyd-Jones. *Courtesy of the Historical Society of the Massapequas.*

Persons Who Have Adhered to the Enemies of This State, and for Declaring the Sovereignty of the People of this State, in Respect to All Property within the Same." The act made clear their futures:

> *That the said several persons herein before particularly named, shall be and hereby are declared to be forever banished from this State; and each and every one of them, who shall at any time hereafter be found in any part*

of this State, shall be, and are hereby adjudged guilty of felony, and shall suffer death in cases of felony, without benefit of clergy.[15]

Jones and his wife left and settled in Hoddesdon, England, where he died in 1792. They were two of the seven thousand exiles who settled in England after the war. He and his wife, Anne, who died in 1817, are buried under the south aisle of Broxbourne Parish Church in Herefordshire.

Judge Jones did not have children, but his father, David, had provided in his will that his property could pass to his daughter Arrabella, a highly unusual provision in an era where male children were automatically deemed heirs of their father's property. The restriction was that she needed her husband to add the name "Jones" in order to maintain the appearance of the property belonging to the Jones family. Arrabella had married Colonel Richard Floyd in 1757. Richard was a cousin of William Floyd, who lived in Mastic and had signed the Declaration of Independence. The legislature approved the terms of David's will, despite the fact that Richard was a Loyalist and later fled to Canada. Richard amended his last name to Floyd-Jones. His and Arrabella's son David Richard, born in 1764, became the inheritor of the Jones property in 1788 upon agreement by the New York State Assembly and took the name David Richard Floyd-Jones. The Floyd-Jones name became the preeminent name in the Massapequas for the next century and a half.

COLD SPRING HARBOR

Several Jones family members remained in the Massapequas, but many moved away, doubtless because of the political differences exposed by the American Revolution. John Jones was the first, settling in Cold Spring Harbor in 1784 and managing a gristmill from 1790. He and his family established businesses and became involved in local politics. One of their most enduring legacies is the beautiful St. John's Church, built on land donated by him in 1837. Located on the west side of a millpond that became known as St. John's Lake, the large white Episcopal church is a striking example of nineteenth-century Gothic architecture. It was under the care of Walter Restored Jones for many years.

St. John's Church became the center of public life for the Joneses, as well as other Episcopalians. There are monuments to various family members on the inside and outside, as well as a family cemetery, set on a hill to the west of the church. Burials were common there throughout the 1800s, but it became neglected by the end of the nineteenth century. There was one burial in 1905 and only one other (Rosalie Jones in 1978) in the twentieth century. The crypt at the top of the hill containing Jones family remains was vandalized in 1970, and it was subsequently sealed.

In 1862, John Divine Jones gave the church thirty-seven acres on the high ground about one mile west of Cold Spring Harbor to create the Memorial Cemetery of St. John's Church in Laurel Hollow. Many parishioners were buried there, along with some local residents. The Jones family used that site for their burials and continued to do so throughout the twentieth century. The large Jones plot is a valuable repository of historical and genealogical information about this important family in Cold Spring Harbor's and Long Island's history.

Three influential Jones family members in Cold Spring Harbor were the two Walter Restored Joneses and Walter Restored Twice Jones. The original Walter Jones was born in 1773 and died at age fourteen. The later Walter, born six years later in 1793 (died 1855), was welcomed by his mother with

Jones family monument at St. John's Cemetery. *Author's collection.*

the comment, "My Walter has been restored to me" and was given the middle name Restored. The second Walter Restored was a cousin born in 1821. The third Walter (Restored Twice, 1830–1906) was another cousin (John H. Jones's son), so named because his parents felt it appropriate to continue the first name of Walter in the family. The Restored name was used also by Jackson and Keziah Jones, whose first son, Richard, lived from 1793 to 1796. When a second son was born in 1797, he was named Richard Restored Jones.[16]

In 1828, Walter Restored Jones became the president of the Atlantic Mutual Insurance Company, created to insure his whaling activities. Walter Restored Twice Jones founded the Jones and Whitlock, later Jones and Johnson Marine Insurance Company, in which the younger Walter Restored became a partner. The latter sold his share in 1845 to A. Foster Higgins. The new Johnson and Higgins Company had become the largest private insurance company in the world by the early twentieth century and lasted until 1997, when it was bought by Marsh and McLennan and exists today as a subsidiary. All four Walters were active in St. John's Church as vestrymen, as well as in the Cold Spring Harbor community.

John Divine Jones took over operation of the Hewlett gristmill from his father-in-law, John Hewlett, who had built it in 1790. He ran it as a profitable business and used it to fund whaling activities. Whaling was a major industry in Cold Spring Harbor until the mid-nineteenth century, and the Jones family were at the heart of it. John H. Jones built a sail loft and a cooperage on the west shore of Cold Spring Harbor, on land today occupied by the Cold Spring Harbor Laboratory. He and his brothers outfitted forty-four whaling ships from about 1835, recruiting crews from all around Long Island and supplying ships and crew members from his Jones and Hewlett General Store. Many ships were away for two to three years and came back laden with whale oil, blubber and skins.

The brothers incorporated in 1838 and bought several ships, including the square-rigged *Sheffield*, the largest ship to ever sail from Long Island and the third-largest whaling ship ever built. Between 1836 and 1862, their nine-vessel fleet made forty-four voyages and returned home with $1.5 million of oil and bone. A typical crew size was twenty-five, and the average age twenty-three. Work was hard and dangerous, discipline was harsh and crews typically divided up one-third of the profits, the other two-thirds going to owners and agents and to maintenance of the ship. The Joneses were the first to sail into the uncharted Bering Sea, hunting whales so far north because they were not so numerous in the Pacific by the mid-1850s.

WHALEMEN WANTED.

Experienced and Green Hands are wanted for the Ship's of the

COLD SPRING WHALING COMPANY

to sail from Cold Spring Harbor, Long Island. Apply immediately to

JOHN H. JONES, Agent.

Cold Spring, 6th July, 1839.

Whaling recruitment poster. *Courtesy of Cold Spring Harbor Whaling Museum.*

Walter Jones and associates controlled the whaling fleet, satisfying the markets for oil, candles and whalebone. His position as head of the Atlantic Mutual Insurance Company put him in an advantageous position when insurance was needed. Cold Spring Harbor whaling activities declined in the 1850s, as Walter died in 1855 and John in 1858. Their descendants were more interested in running the various stores and commercial ventures they had established and ended the whaling business. The entire industry collapsed in the 1860s as the Civil War made sailing in American waters treacherous and oil was being discovered and refined in Western Pennsylvania.

The Jones family remained important in Cold Spring Harbor into the twentieth century. John D. Jones established the still-thriving Cold Spring Harbor Fish Hatchery in 1882. The Jones and Hewlett General Store burned in 1896, destroying many of the whaling records stored there. The gristmill burned in 1921, around the same time that other mills that were used to produce woolens that were shipped to New York City, as well as lumber used for local construction, closed down. The largest house in the area was the fifty-room Jones Manor, built in 1868. It burned in 1910 and was replaced by a similar structure that still stands, about one mile south of St. John's Church.[17]

Walter Restored Jones was involved in an unexpected but highly commendable activity. In 1848, he led other investors in forming the Life Saving Benevolent Association, chartered to recognize and reward heroic water rescues, first in the New York area and eventually nationwide. The association joined with the recently established United States Life-Saving Service to create stations along the Atlantic coast, including twenty-six in the New York area, equipped with rescue boats, ropes and lights and staffed by trained lifesavers who would go into the Atlantic to rescue passengers. Many boats foundered in the sandbar located about one quarter mile south of Long Island's beaches, and the lifesavers used whatever tools they had to rescue as many as possible.

Between 1839 and 1848 alone, there were 338 shipwrecks along the coasts of Long Island and New Jersey. Jones was well aware of the hazardous waters surrounding Long Island because of his management of the whaling business and his position in the Atlantic Mutual Insurance Company. He financed construction and distribution of a large and heavy iron lifeboat trailed by a lifecar built by Joseph Francis, credited with saving thousands of lives in the first few years of its use. The Life Saving Benevolent Association exists today and continues to award medals and financial gifts, as well as giving grants to organizations that promote water safety. Its administrative activities were taken over by the Seaman's Church in 2013, and its records are kept at Queens College of the City University of New York.[18]

John Henry Jones took it upon himself to write a genealogy of his ancestors, beginning with Thomas and including families into which the Joneses married, such as Hewlett, Gardiner and Livingston. The volume shows how influential the Joneses were in Long Island's commerce and politics and how widespread their interests were. John H. Jones died in 1905, and his relatives published his work in 1907 with the title *The Jones Family of Long Island: Descendants of Major Thomas Jones (1665–1713) and Allied Families.*

ROSALIE AND MARY JONES

One of the most colorful Jones family members was Rosalie Gardiner Jones, born in 1883, the daughter of Mary and Oliver Jones. Rosalie was an independent and strong-willed woman who came of age as the women's suffrage movement was gaining steam. She led several marches demanding voting rights, including a 170-mile walk to Albany in December 1912 and another to Washington, D.C., in 1913, demonstrating during Woodrow Wilson's inauguration. For her leadership, she earned the nickname "General" Jones. She later earned a law degree from Brooklyn Law School and became the first woman to receive a Doctorate of Civil Law from American University in 1922.

Rosalie Jones kept animals on her Cold Spring Harbor property, defending the practice by using English common law to show that she had no obligation to fence in chickens, dogs, cats, sheep and other small animals. She allowed animals into her house—once a goat jumped out the second-floor window and unfortunately hanged itself on its leash. She built shacks on a piece of land she owned on Eaton's Neck and rented them to low-income people, in defiance of community practices. She also repaired automobiles on the street in front of her house, defying local ordinances that forbade such a practice. Her bitterest defeat was when Robert Moses seized some of her property for a parkway. She argued unsuccessfully against his use of the doctrine of eminent domain.

Rosalie Jones lived a long and colorful life as the maverick of the "Cold Spring Harbor Joneses." She achieved notoriety in 1922 for selling a parcel of land on the water to Walter Abrams, who later sold it to Socony Oil, which erected twelve oil tanks along Shore Road, compromising the beauty of the coastal view. According to local legend, Rosalie was displeased because the Cold Spring Harbor Beach Club had not invited the Jones family to join. The tanks remained until 2005, so her name lived on for many years. The oil tank site is owned currently by the North Shore Land Alliance.[19]

Rosalie died in 1978 and requested that her ashes be scattered in front of the Jones family crypt located at the old St. John's Cemetery. She also requested a stone be erected outside the family crypt. She was interred in a cemetery that had seen its last interment in 1905, rather than the Jones family plot in the Memorial Cemetery. This was interpreted as one more example of her independent spirit and her discomfort with the values of her relatives.

Mary Gardiner Jones, Rosalie's niece, was another remarkable Jones woman, if not as bizarre as her aunt. Her mother, in fact, told her, "Don't grow up like your aunt Rosalie." Born in 1922, she worked in the Office of Strategic Services (later the CIA) during World War II and went to law school after the war. She became the first woman to receive a degree from

Rosalie Gardiner Jones. *Courtesy of Library of Congress Photo Collection.*

Yale Law School in 1948 and the first to be hired by a major Washington, D.C., law firm. The firm was Donovan and Leisure and was headed by General "Wild Bill" Donovan, who founded the OSS and was familiar with Mary's talents. This connection was crucial because she was turned down by more than a dozen law firms in the D.C. area, who refused to hire a woman.

Mary became involved in consumer-related activities, just as these were becoming important public issues. Appointed the first female commissioner of the Federal Trade Commission by Lyndon Johnson, she succeeded in having cigarette advertisements banned from radio, television and print and mandated inclusion of care instructions on all clothing sold in the United States.

Mary Gardiner Jones went to work in private business after the FTC and held several important leadership posts. Upon her retirement, she became involved in issues relating to children and senior citizens in Washington, D.C., establishing the D.C. Mental Health Institute. She published an autobiography, *Tearing Down Walls: One Woman's Triumph*, in 2007. She never married or had children and, upon her death in 2009, became the last surviving Jones family member. She is buried at the Memorial Cemetery of St. John's Church, but not in the Jones family plot. She had never become comfortable with the family's wealth and her relatives' constant squabbling over property ownership and directed that she be buried in her mother's family's plot.[20]

Several Jones descendants, many from an earlier era, are buried at a small cemetery on Merrick Road just east of Massapequa Avenue called Jones Cemetery (also West Neck Cemetery). There are forty-one stones and remnants of several others in the western half of the cemetery. Sixty-one, most from the eastern half, were moved in 1892 when the Floyd-Jones Cemetery opened behind Old Grace Church.[21]

Among those buried in West Neck is Colonel Benjamin Birdsall (1736–1798), who fought in the Revolutionary War. He was involved in hiding food supplies, cattle and grain from the British, thus disrupting their supply lines. He was arrested and later released. After the war, he served in the New York State Assembly. A plaque in his honor was erected in the cemetery by the Ruth Floyd Woodhull Chapter of the Daughters of the American Revolution.

Another notable Jones family member buried in the West Neck Cemetery is Samuel Jones (1734–1819), a member of the assembly in the 1780s who was responsible for convincing other members to vote for ratification of the new Constitution. Ten states had ratified by 1788, but New York held out because of concerns over central government power. Worried that New York could convince the three other holdouts to challenge the creation of the United States, Jones persuaded opponents to vote by proposing a Bill of Rights that would enumerate powers appropriate to the federal government and those reserved for the states. Jones later became the New York City recorder, a state senator and the state comptroller. A memorial stone was erected at the West Neck Cemetery in his honor in 1988 by the Historical Society of the Massapequas.

A few Jones family members remained in the Massapequas (called then South Oyster Bay) and owned large parcels of property but did not have the local influence of the more numerous and established Floyd-Jones family members. A 1914 map shows John Jones owning a large part of what became northern Massapequa Park. His influence, and that of his relatives, shrank steadily in South Oyster Bay after 1900.

Chapter 4

THE FLOYD-JONESES
SHAPE THE MASSAPEQUAS

The split within the Jones family after the American Revolution left the southeastern corner of what became Nassau County almost exclusively to the Floyd-Jones family. David Richard was granted the six thousand acres that were enumerated in David Jones's will in 1788, and Captain Thomas Floyd-Jones subsequently inherited them as one parcel in 1826, according to the existing law of entailment, which gave property to the eldest surviving son. That law was overturned in 1832, when the inheritance laws were rewritten to make inheritance a more family-related matter. That meant several children of one parent could inherit property, which happened in 1851 when Thomas passed away and his property was divided equally among his four children: David Richard, William, Elbert and Sarah Maria. They and their relatives were active in politics, holding several positions in New York State. Most dramatically, they proceeded to build estates on their property, setting the tone for the development of the Massapequas for the next century.

MANSIONS AND RESIDENTS[22]

Thomas Jones's Old Brick House was the forerunner of the many mansions along Merrick Road owned by Floyd-Jones family members. A later observer captured this transition: "On the east side of the Massapequa River stood the Old Brick House, which withstanding the storms of 140 years, was taken down in 1837. The Indian trail became a tree-lined country road where descendants lived in fine houses." Thomas Jones's brick house had remained empty for many years as his family grew and developed. The younger generations who became involved in law or business built year-round houses in Lower Manhattan in the area east of Washington Square known as Fort Pitt. Current street names such as Jones Street, Jones Alley and Great Jones Street reflect their presence. The large parcel of land originally owned by Thomas Jones, as well as the Fort Neck House (the post-Revolution name of Tryon Hall), doubtless attracted them, and they began to build estates in the area, then known variously as Fort Neck or South Oyster Bay.

All but one of South Oyster Bay's fine mansions were built in the nineteenth century. The oldest was built by a Jones because the Floyd-Jones name did not exist at the time. That was Tryon Hall, built in 1770 by David Jones for his son Thomas, then a Tory judge. It was the largest building in the area, ninety feet long, consisting of thirty rooms, overlooking South Oyster Bay, but with the main entrance facing northward. It consisted of three floors, with a large entrance hall thirty-six feet long by twenty-three feet wide, floored in southern pine. It was located on the south side of Kings Highway (later South Country Road and then Merrick Road), one hundred feet north of where Merrick Road stands today.

David Jones, son of the original Thomas, had moved into the Old Brick House upon its completion but made it clear to his son Thomas, who was destined to inherit his property, that he should live in South Oyster Bay rather than in New York City. David deeded the large house to Thomas in 1773. Thomas moved there and became owner of the mansion and of his father's property when David died in October 1775, six months after the beginning of the American Revolution. It was the first and for many years the only large estate in the Massapequas. It stood west of where Massapequa High School is today.

Tryon Hall was named after William Tryon, governor of New York, another example of Thomas and his father David's political leanings. It was a spacious building. To the left of the entrance hall was a freestanding stair that was noted by everybody who entered. There was also a drawing room, a library, a kitchen and a formal dining room on the first floor. There were five bedrooms upstairs and servants' rooms on the third floor. Thomas, by then a judge, used Tryon Hall to entertain fellow supporters of the king and also allowed them to stay there for their safety, earning the name "Refugee House."

Tryon Hall was renamed Fort Neck House after the Revolution and was occupied by several generations of Floyd-Joneses, beginning with David Richard. It was considered a remarkable structure because of the main staircase, which was built out from the wall without any apparent supports. As the building aged, it became too large and cumbersome for family members to maintain. It remained in the family until 1920, when George Stanton Floyd-Jones sold it to the Corroon family, who ran it as a hotel for about ten years. Electricity and indoor plumbing were added about 1900, but the house looked more and more anachronistic as the area became more populated.

We are fortunate to have detailed drawings and photos of the empty building, done as a Civilian Conservation Corps project in the mid-1930s. The Nassau County Historical Society published a proposal to take control of the building and turn it into a museum. Discussions were held with Nassau County and Town of Oyster Bay officials, but no resolution was reached. Sadly, the Fort Neck House suffered the same fate as many other old and abandoned buildings. A fire, apparently accidental, set it ablaze on October 1940, and the building was reduced to rubble in a few hours. The building was empty, so there was no memorabilia destroyed. What was there was removed many years before and may be in private hands today. The author recently saw a set of antlers that may have hung in the main hall.

A traveler going east along Merrick Road in the mid-nineteenth century (at that time called South Country Road) would have encountered just a few large houses on the way to Amityville. The westernmost mansion along Merrick Road was built by an owner who was peripherally connected to the Floyd-Jones family. The Willow House, later termed the Red House, was built just to the east of Tackapausha Preserve (the western boundary of the Massapequas) by James Meinell, a millionaire leather manufacturer who also owned the New American Theatre on lower Broadway in New York City. He was a member of Grace Church and served as its treasurer in the 1850s. He died in a construction accident in 1865, and his family continued to live in the house until 1890, when it became a tourist home and summer hotel. It was sold in 1922 to the Masone family, who owned it until 1942. It aged significantly in the next twenty years and was torn down in 1964, one of the many fine structures destroyed as the Massapequas became a heavily populated suburb.

Our eastbound traveler would have next seen the Van De Water Hotel on Hicksville Road (built in 1796) and Massapequa Manor, to the east of West Neck Cemetery. In 1837, David Jones built the manor, an imposing structure on the east bank of Massapequa Lake. He was responsible for creating the one-hundred-acre lake, dredging out a swampy area with two streams to create a large body of water that could be used for boating, fishing and other leisure pursuits. He created an island in the middle of the lake, named Mary's Island after his third wife, Mary Clinton, daughter of Governor DeWitt Clinton.

Massapequa Manor was approached from Merrick Road along a circular driveway and featured five large Greek-style columns and a spacious wraparound porch. There were outbuildings for horses, chickens and other animals, as well as for the caretakers who maintained the property and servants who cared for the family. The property ran several acres north and east and featured a windmill, barns and a racetrack, which was popular for several years in the mid-nineteenth century. A large boathouse was used for family gatherings and significant events. It had a stone fireplace, a kitchen, an area for dancing and a deck with railings. This was the second mansion built by Thomas Jones's descendants.[23]

The next mansion, moving eastward, was Sedgmoor, near Dover Road today, built in 1854 by Sarah Maria Floyd-Jones, daughter of Brigadier General Thomas Floyd-Jones. She received a portion of her father's estate

Massapequa Manor. *Courtesy of the Historical Society of the Massapequas.*

because he had died intestate—that is, without a will—and his heirs, three sons and one daughter, were granted equal parts of his holdings. After her father's death in 1851, Ms. Floyd-Jones married Coleman Williams, who was later instrumental in establishing the Old Grace Church Cemetery and the Floyd-Jones Cemetery. Their property extended from Merrick Road north to the area around Sunrise Highway and east to where Old Grace Church stands today. Sedgmoor was a three-story wooden structure facing Merrick Road, encircled by an enclosed porch and topped off by a large tower. Little is known about the interior, but it was a very somber building, with a walkway in the front, trees on each side and a cleared field in the back. Coleman Williams Jr. inherited Sedgmoor upon his father Coleman Williams Sr.'s death in 1891. He was Sarah Maria Floyd-Jones's husband. Williams Jr. died in 1900, and his wife, Edith Hawley, married John Oddie in 1905. Sedgmoor became known commonly as the Oddie House and remained standing until 1953.

Mr. Williams donated a portion of his property east of Sedgmoor to Old Grace Church, which, thanks to an 1884 New York State law, was permitted to build a cemetery on its adjacent property. He also laid out the Floyd-Jones Cemetery behind Grace Church Cemetery in 1892, separating the two by a hedge, which is currently six feet tall. The latter cemetery extended back to Beaumont Avenue. He also donated property to build the Floyd-Jones Library in 1896, showing the extent of his father's and his generosity.

Another mansion was built directly across from Sedgmoor, namely Holland House, completed around 1890 by Ella Floyd-Jones and her husband, William Carpender. The house was relatively modest, with a long driveway leading up from Merrick Road, but it rested on property that stretched down to South Oyster Bay. William Carpender was an avid fisherman and often took neighbors and their sons with him on his boat. Ralph Wiley, son of Grace Church's longtime rector, William Wiley, described several of these trips in humorous fashion in his autobiography, *Preacher's Son*.

Holland House was sold by the family after Mr. Carpender's death in 1927 and turned into the Wagon Wheel Restaurant, which became very popular for many years. By the early 1950s, the Massapequas were experiencing a huge population boom, and the Roman Catholic Diocese of Brooklyn was searching for a place to build a church. The diocese purchased the restaurant and the property in 1952 and used it for Mass and as a rectory. St. Rose of Lima School was completed in 1956, and the church was finally completed in 1965. The Wagon Wheel was then torn down, and the site is today St. Rose's parking lot.

Left: Holland House. *Courtesy of the Historical Society of the Massapequas.*

Below: Wagon Wheel restaurant, 1930s. *Courtesy of the Historical Society of the Massapequas.*

It's noteworthy that Holland House had a servants' cottage behind and to the left, at the eastern end of William Street. That structure was purchased by the Collamore family when the Wagon Wheel was opened and still stands today. It closely resembles the Floyd-Jones servants' cottage, which stands in Massapequa's Historic Complex. The latter building was completed in 1870 as an outbuilding to the Elbert Floyd-Jones mansion near Harbor Lane and Merrick Road. Like other Floyd-Jones estates, these buildings housed servants who cared for the family and who made up a large part of the local population through the nineteenth century.

Elbert Floyd-Jones was a significant member of the Floyd-Jones family. He was a New York State assemblyman on two occasions and was the guiding light behind construction of Old Grace Church. He built his mansion east of Holland House in 1870. It was a simple and severe-looking building that housed his fourth wife and his family. She remained in the house after his death in 1901 and lived there until her death in 1918. The building was left vacant and burned in 1926, apparently as the result of a fireworks explosion on July 4. The servants' cottage became a rental property until the 1970s, when it was abandoned. The Historical Society of the Massapequas moved it across Merrick Road to its present location in Massapequa's Historic Complex in 1986.

Fort Neck, described earlier, was the next house east on Merrick Road. Just east of that was Sewan (the Native American term for shell beads), built around 1885. Many observers consider it the most attractive of the Floyd-Jones mansions. It had a bright and cheerful look, facing Merrick Road (which was relocated south to its current location by then), and was fronted by a large landscaped yard and adorned with flowers on all sides. It was the first house in the Massapequas to have indoor plumbing.

George Stanton Floyd-Jones, its owner, became very successful in the insurance business, working his way to the position of secretary of the Atlantic Mutual Insurance Company, founded by Walter Restored Jones. He became involved in local issues, financing the construction of a large Victorian train station in 1890 to replace the small, plain building that was erected by the railroad in 1886. He felt that Massapequa deserved a station befitting its stature.

Floyd-Jones later participated in discussions that led to the creation of the Massapequa Water District. Local residents had petitioned the Town of Oyster Bay in 1927 to create a separate water district to serve the growing population. He opposed the additional tax that would be imposed, wondering why he should pay for water that he was currently pumping from

Sewan. *Courtesy of the Historical Society of the Massapequas.*

his own wells. His situation was clearly unique, as few residents possessed either the money or equipment to locate and/or pump groundwater. After several meetings with Floyd-Jones and other local representatives, the town decided in 1931 to create a Water District with the responsibility to develop a piping and storage system that would provide water throughout the area.

Town officials respected Mr. Floyd-Jones's concerns by exempting him and other large landowners in the southeastern part of the Massapequas from joining the district. Later homeowners who were unable and unwilling to pump their own water contracted with the American Water Works Company (now known as New York American Water) to provide water service.[24]

George Stanton Floyd-Jones left his mark on several other features of the area. He was David Richard II's son, born in 1848. Along with two of his sisters, Mary and Henrietta, he founded St. Michael and All Angels Episcopal Church in Seaford. In 1894, he became a Roman Catholic, as was his wife, Anita, breaking with the Episcopalian affiliation of both the Jones and Floyd-Jones families. He was involved in creating the Floyd-Jones Cemetery and caused a stir among his relatives when he paid for a crucifix installed in the back of the cemetery. The crucifix shows Jesus Christ hanging on the cross, something Episcopalians do not accept. Their vision, and that of most Protestants, centers on the Resurrection, and their crosses are usually bright and uplifting, not showing Jesus's sufferings.

George Stanton Floyd-Jones was a nattily dressed man, always appearing at the Massapequa train station with highly polished shoes. According to Ralph Wiley, "His neatly pressed striped trousers were surmounted by a swallow-tail coat, wing collar and cravat. A generous white moustache was

George Stanton Floyd-Jones. *Courtesy of the Historical Society of the Massapequas.*

neatly waxed with points elevated at a jaunty angle. All this was topped with a square-topped derby."[25]

George's wife died in 1940, and he passed one year later. In his will, he gave Sewan to the Dominican Sisters, who used it as their residence and ran it as Queen of the Rosary Academy from 1948 until 1952. The building and grounds were then bought by the Massapequa School District, torn down and replaced by Massapequa High School.

George Stanton Floyd-Jones left a unique memorial that the historical society has preserved. In the 1890s, bicycling became very popular, and cyclists and horses crowded along Merrick Road. To provide some comfort in the hot weather, Floyd-Jones installed a water pump, with a separate trough for horses and a tin cup for cyclists, near where Burns Park is today. He had a sign cut into a stone which read

Stay, weary traveler, rest a awhile,
No banquet this nor merry feast,
But here will flow at thy desire
Pure water for both man and beast.
George Stanton Floyd-Jones.

A smaller stone, marked "For the Horse," currently stands to the right of the Floyd-Jones servants' cottage, facing the entrance, in Massapequa's Historic Complex.[26]

Unqua, also known as Rosedale, was built by Henry Floyd-Jones in the 1840s and was east of Sewan. It was a large and rather plain two-story building facing a lowland that later became John Burns Park. Floyd-Jones died in 1862, and his wife, Helen, lived there until her death in 1872. It was owned by Edward Floyd-Jones and sold by his wife after his death in 1930. The new owners lived on the property until after World War II, when it was torn down and replaced by a shopping center that features Ace Hardware today. The area behind it was where the Arlen Oaks development grew.

Little Unqua is one of the more interesting of the Jones/Floyd-Jones mansions. The Native American word *unqua* means "far away," and it was so named because it was the most easterly of the family's mansions. It was "little" only because it was smaller than the larger Unqua mansion to the

Unqua. *Courtesy of the Historical Society of the Massapequas.*

west. Little Unqua was built in 1861 by Edward Floyd-Jones, who was a New York State senator and later Queens County supervisor. In 1867, his daughter, Louise, was born and inherited the mansion and property when she married Conde Thorn in 1889. Her husband died in 1944, and she remained on her estate until her death in 1961.

We don't have detailed information about most of Massapequa's mansions, but we know quite a bit about Little Unqua thanks to the efforts of former Historical Society trustee Barbara Fisher, who interviewed John Nolan, who had worked on the estate as a teenager in 1958. He described the house as large, with two sets of porches, one over the other, painted a grayish blue. The building faced Merrick Road just west of Unqua Road. There was a circular driveway in front that led in from the Unqua-Merrick corner and exited to the west near Unqua Lake. To the right of the house was a formal garden with cedar trees and a variety of flowers and plants. A barn and a stable were situated at the northwest, near the lake. A paddock with horses was located toward the rear of the property, and a quarter-mile riding track was maintained at the northeast corner.[27]

Toward the end of her life, Louise Floyd-Jones Thorn became the center of a multifaceted discussion concerning her property. By the late 1950s, the Massapequas were developing rapidly, and every bit of empty space was being filled or repurposed. Several proposals were made for Little Unqua:

- a school
- a hospital
- an art museum
- single-family houses
- apartments
- a shopping center

All of these proposals were appropriate on their face, but the interested parties had to contend with Mrs. Thorn's occupancy of Little Unqua. She had expressed her disdain at the development of the Massapequas and felt that a park of some sort should replace her estate, but only after her death.

Into this difficult situation stepped another notable woman: Marjorie Rankin Post. Her family had moved from New Jersey in 1922, when her father was named postmaster of the Massapequas. She was named Massapequa's first female postmistress (delivering mail on horseback in her early years) and subsequently became involved in operating an insurance and real estate company. She also worked as school secretary

Possible Layout of Thorn Estate
As Suggested by Oral History.
Not drawn to Scale:

FARM LAND

BARN Stable AREA ORCHARD RACE TRACK PRESENT GATE

Paddeck

WELL 2 CAR GARAGE GARdNER'S CoTTAGE

LAKE

GARdEN PORCHES HOUSE

DRIVE WAY

SASSAFRAS GROVE UNGUA ROAD

LAWN

PEdESTRIAN GATE RodedendRum Bush

DAM MERRICK ROAD BEECH TREES

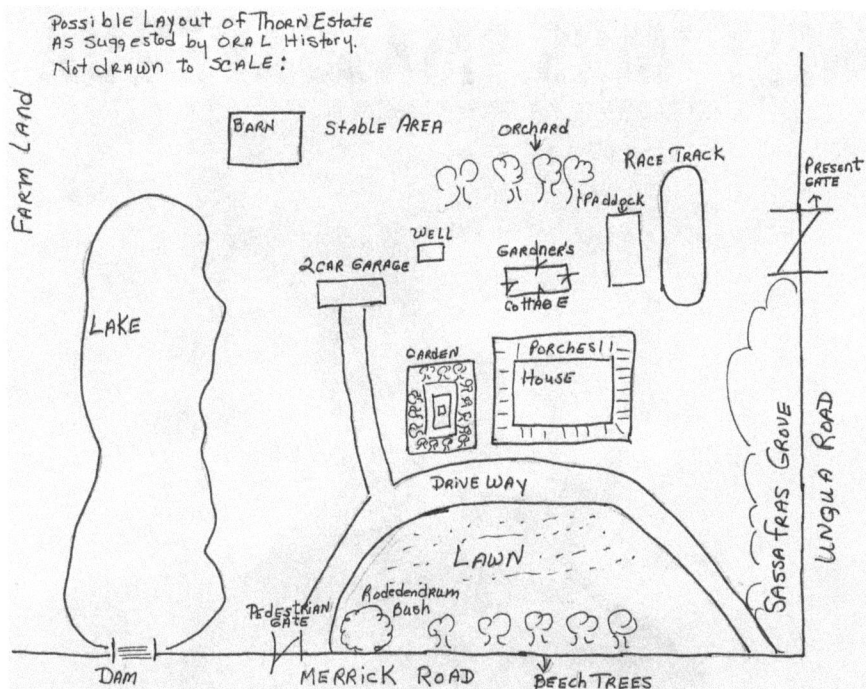

Little Unqua (Thorn estate) grounds. *Courtesy of the Historical Society of the Massapequas.*

and drove ambulances during World War II, ferrying wounded sailors from the Brooklyn Navy Yard to a hospital located at Mitchell Field. She was appointed to a vacant seat on the Oyster Bay Town Council in 1957, becoming the town's first councilwoman. She knew Louise Floyd-Jones Thorn and sided with her in her wish to change Little Unqua into a park. Her political lobbying paid off after Mrs. Thorn's death in 1961, because Oyster Bay's town council voted to purchase the forty-two-acre property, tear down the building and construct a park with three swimming pools, handball and tennis courts, picnic grounds, playgrounds and ample parking. Upon its completion in 1965, the park was named for Marjorie Post.

Kaycroft was an original Jones mansion, built by Walter Restored Jones in the mid-1850s in northern Massapequa and moved to its location at the corner of Merrick and Unqua Roads in the early 1900s. It was remodeled and occupied by Katherine Jones Whipple. By the mid-1900s, it, too, had become an expense for its owners and was bought by developers, who tore it down in 1965 and built a nursing home on the location. There was some

MEET 'MRS. MASSAPEQUA'

Marjorie Rankin Post. *Courtesy of the Historical Society of the Massapequas.*

discussion of moving it to Old Bethpage Village Restoration, which was created in 1963 to save older structures that were vanishing rapidly, but that never happened.

The easternmost mansion in the Massapequas was the Baldwin-Hilbert House, a Victorian structure built bordering County Line Road. The original owner is unidentified, but it was purchased in 1873 by Timothy Baldwin, a Civil War veteran, and sold in 1947 to Dr. Kenneth Hilbert, a veterinarian who owned it until 1992. The building exhibited gingerbread trim in the front and was three stories high, with six gabled dormers and a large front porch. The two-and-a-half-acre site had a pond and rose and perennial gardens.[28]

The Baldwin-Hilbert House had pheasants, peacocks and spotted fallow deer in the back, in keeping with Dr. Hilbert's veterinary profession. He was a world-renowned expert on poultry diseases and director of the Poultry Laboratory at Farmingdale State University. He was also busy caring for the many animals kept at Frank Buck's Zoo and later the Massapequa Zoo. His son Stuart sold the house in 1992, and the buyers pledged to restore the house. However, a series of "misunderstandings" led to the house's destruction in 1996, ending the era of Massapequa's grand mansions. In keeping with the long-standing pattern of building several structures on old estate sites, the property is now occupied by County Line Villas.

OLD GRACE CHURCH

Elbert Floyd-Jones, mentioned earlier, was also instrumental in building Grace Church in the midst of the Floyd-Jones mansions. He and his family members found it tedious to make the fifteen-mile trip to St. George's Episcopal Church in Hempstead for worship services in the 1840s. Back then, there were no paved roads and no trains, so the trip had to be made by horse-drawn wagon along South Country Road, in the heat and rain of the summer months. Throughout 1844, Elbert requested support from other family members, fellow Episcopalians and churches in Babylon, Islip, Brooklyn and New York City. His efforts resulted in a fund of $1,300, to be used for drawings, land clearing, materials and construction.

Elbert and his family built their church on the north side of Merrick Road, made of wood and with a brick foundation and a marble altar. Plans were made to commission stained-glass windows from a master craftsman. Female members of the family discussed plans to make tapestries for the building. The original building was a square structure with clapboard siding and diamond stained-glass windows. The simple model was taken from a candle box and is replicated in St. Andrew's Episcopal Church in Yaphank, built in 1853. The building had an arched roof made of wooden timbers. It

Grace Church and Wiley Hall, circa 1950. *Courtesy of the Historical Society of the Massapequas.*

resembles the bottom of a ship, and some have speculated it was designed that way in honor of Thomas Jones's privateering activities. There is no record that this was the intent. A large window designed by the English firm of Heaton, Butler and Bayne was installed behind the altar in 1862 in memory of Thomas Floyd-Jones (1788–1851) and Henry Onderdonk Floyd-Jones (1792–1862).

Henry Floyd-Jones was named chair, and Thomas Lawrence and Thomas Floyd-Jones were named wardens of the new church. Elbert became one of the vestrymen. It was completed in 1845 and consecrated in April 1847. The first recorded event was a funeral for twenty-one-year-old Eliza Kortright in July 1845. The first marriage was in 1849 and was one of very few in the early years because marriages were usually conducted in private homes, especially the large and ornate structures owned by the Floyd-Joneses. Several baptisms were held, but two early confirmations took place in New York City because of the difficulty of having the bishop travel to such a remote area.[29]

Grace Church after 1905 renovation. *Courtesy of the Historical Society of the Massapequas.*

Old Grace Church's early years were quite rocky. Several temporary pastors were employed until a permanent pastor could be found because the church was only opened during the summer months. The Floyd-Joneses, as well as the Joneses, lived and worked in Lower Manhattan during the colder months and provided meager financial support for a resident priest. S. Stebbins Stocking was the first full-time rector, appointed in 1867. He served until 1890, when Reverend William Wiley was appointed. He served until 1926 and was responsible for the church's expansion and modernization, as well as the creation of St. Christopher's Chapel in North Massapequa.

By the turn of the century, more than one hundred Floyd-Jones family members and their servants resided in the area. There were also settlers in Stadt Wurttemberg (Massapequa Park today) and North Massapequa. The number of Grace Church communicants had grown from 23 in the 1850s to 68 in 1891 and 153 by 1919. The vestry in 1905 accepted Father Wiley's recommendation to modernize and expand the church and built a new entrance in the front, topped by a steeple and featuring two side doors with porticos. They brought electricity into the building and installed a heating system. The Long Island Railroad had made it easier for residents to live in the area year-round and commute to New York City, hence the need for a heating system in a church that was initially opened only during the summers. After 1907, it remained in use throughout the year.

FLOYD-JONES FAMILY MEMBERS

Delancey Floyd-Jones was the most notable Floyd-Jones family member. Ironically, he never owned an estate in the Massapequas. He was born in 1826, the son of Henry Onderdonk Floyd-Jones, who was a major general in the Queens County Militia. He entered West Point in 1842 and was the only Jones or Floyd-Jones family member to graduate from a military academy. He was an acceptable student, finishing forty-fifth out of sixty students but finishing in the top third in engineering. Upon graduation, he was sent to fight in the Mexican-American War, a proving ground for many West Point graduates who would later use their experiences in the American Civil War.

Delancey Floyd-Jones remained in the army after the Mexican-American War, receiving several assignments during the Indian Wars, including fighting in the Rogue Wars, which strengthened the United States' grip in the area that later became the states of Oregon and Washington. When the Civil War began, he held the rank of major and was assigned to aid in recruiting in New England and to guard the Port of Boston. He was one of very few soldiers from the Mexican-American War who had remained in the army, which consisted of about five thousand men in 1861.

Floyd-Jones's greatest claim to fame came in 1863 at Gettysburg, where he was assigned after fighting in the Virginia Peninsular Campaign of 1862. His Eleventh Infantry Regiment was responsible for defending the Wheatfield. Confederate forces were advancing from the south and aiming to gain the high ground and sweep through Gettysburg. They planned then to turn east and march toward Maryland and Washington, D.C. Floyd-Jones and his Fifth Corps held the Wheatfield through July 2–3, stopping the Confederate advance.

Floyd-Jones began the battle with 25 officers and 281 men; 15 officers were killed or wounded, as were 101 soldiers. He fought bravely and skillfully and was promoted to brevet colonel. His military record notes that he was promoted "for gallant and meritorious service at Gettysburg." His 1902 obituary notice quoted Lieutenant General George Sykes, who recommended him for the promotion:

> As commander of the Fifth Corps, I had the opportunity to observe the zeal of Colonel Floyd-Jones in the campaign and battle of Gettysburg, and for those special instances and his services during the rebellion, respectfully recommend him for the brevet of Brigadier General in the army.[30]

There is a stone at Gettysburg honoring him, located on a small hillock with about ten other memorials. The area is designated for career soldiers like Floyd-Jones, of whom there were very few when the Civil War began.

One month after Gettysburg, Floyd-Jones was formally promoted to lieutenant colonel and assigned to defend the fortifications at Fort Independence, Massachusetts, and later to defend Boston Harbor, his earlier assignment. He remained at Boston until the end of the war. In the next three years, he was assigned to a variety of commands and eventually was promoted to brigadier general in 1868.

Delancey remained in the army at the end of the war and was given command of several locations, ranging from Detroit to Little Rock, Idaho, to Holly Springs, Mississippi, and Jackson Barracks, Louisiana. He served as superintendent of Indian affairs, as a recruiter, as an inspector general and judge advocate and was involved in putting down railroad disturbances in

Pennsylvania. He seems to have been somebody who could be assigned to a variety of activities and perform them well. His military record indicates that he "retired from active service upon his own application, Mar. 20, 1879, having served over thirty years."

In the years after the Civil War, Floyd-Jones traveled extensively throughout the world, using his service time to take extended leaves of absence. The Queensborough Public Library's archives have several scrapbooks containing letters he sent back to Long Island, most to his sister Kate (Josephine Katherine, 1832–1905), as well as articles he wrote for local newspapers. He recorded his first trip, to several European cities and to Tangiers, from March to November 1868. A second trip, from June 1875 until February 1876, found him in Europe as well as in Egypt. In this instance, he sent back dispatches to the *Hempstead Inquirer* using the name "Au Revoir." After he left the army, he traveled throughout Europe in 1881 and 1882.

His most extensive trip was an around-the-world voyage from October 1885 until June 1886. He traveled through Europe, Egypt, India, China and Japan and ended his narrative in San Francisco, detailing his experiences in letters to Amityville's *South Side Signal*. He wrote these letters under the name "Unqua," which he described as his "Country Place in Oyster Bay." This was the home of his brother Edward Floyd-Jones, located on Merrick Road across from today's Burns Park.

Floyd-Jones collected and edited these letters and published them in 1887 as *Letters from the Far East*, detailing his experiences, which took far longer than those described by Jules Verne in *Around the World in Eighty Days* (published in 1873 and referenced by Floyd-Jones). He traveled first class on the newest ships, stayed at the best hotels, ate at Officers' Clubs or at restaurants recommended by local officials and visited with Americans living in European and Asian cities. He toured famous sites such as the pyramids, the Taj Mahal and the Yangtze River and wrote positive reviews of most of his experiences. The book provides pleasant and enjoyable reading and was generally well received when published, except for a negative review printed by the *Washington Post* on June 26, 1887: "The narrative is very plain and exceedingly matter of fact. Col. Jones evidently traveled for enjoyment, and not for study or observation. The book has no special merit." Despite that review, the book sold very well, especially among present and former military personnel.

Colonel Floyd-Jones traveled alone, despite the fact that he had married Minnie Oglesby in 1878. They had apparently lived separately for many years. His first wife, Laura Whitney, died in September 1852, three months after they were married. He had no children, and there is no record he ever built or owned an estate, as did most of his family members. He appears to have lived at the Union Club in New York City and to have stayed with his brother Edward at Unqua during the warm weather. His name, however, remains on the library he created to serve the residents living along the south shore.

DELANCEY FLOYD-JONES FREE LIBRARY

In 1896, Floyd-Jones convinced Coleman Williams, his cousin, to donate a small parcel of property east of Grace Church, on which he built a one-room library. The building cost $1,500 and was heated by a fireplace in the middle. There is no record that the library was lit by electricity when it was built, but that was added in the early twentieth century. His relatives donated a table, chairs and bookcases, all of which are still in use. They also donated books and paid for the services of a librarian. The library was open to the public five days each week, with an interesting twist. Any patron could buy a key for ten dollars that allowed entry to the building at any time—for taking out or returning books, for reading or for meeting with friends and other patrons. One of the original keys is still on display in the library, which stands on its original site on Merrick Road across from Cedar Shore Drive.

The Delancey Floyd-Jones Library became exceedingly popular, first among family members and then with people who settled the area in the late nineteenth and early twentieth centuries. Its namesake doubtless took great satisfaction from this, but it was short-lived. He died in New York City from pneumonia on January 19, 1902, one day before his seventy-sixth birthday. He was buried in the Floyd-Jones family plot behind Old Grace Church, leaving a legacy of extensive military service and a library that endures to this day.

Another significant Floyd-Jones military person was Brigadier General Thomas Floyd-Jones (1778–1851). He commanded the militia assembled at Fort Greene in Brooklyn in the War of 1812 and is listed as captain. The militia's muster rolls are located in the Floyd-Jones Library. He is also noteworthy as the last Floyd-Jones family member to hold Thomas Jones's full estate by inheritance. An 1832 law abolished the law of entail, giving him possession in what is called fee simple. He was thus able to divide his

Above: Delancey Floyd-Jones Free Library, 1907. *Courtesy of Delancey Floyd-Jones Free Library.*

Right: Sister Henrietta Floyd-Jones Window. *Author's collection.*

estate into four equal parts of 1,200 acres, with each of his four children receiving their parcel upon his death in 1851.

Several Floyd-Jones family members were important in New York politics also. Elbert Floyd-Jones was an assemblyman on two different occasions. His brother David Richard Floyd-Jones II was lieutenant governor and secretary of state. Edward Floyd-Jones was a state senator, and Henry Onderdonk Floyd-Jones was an assemblyman and state senator. They were active in the first half of the nineteenth century, but later generations did not follow them into politics. Elbert's son, in fact, also named Elbert, became the longtime pastor of St. Mary of the Highlands Church in Cold Spring, New York, holding that position until his death in 1947. David Richard's daughter Henrietta became an Episcopal nun, joining the Sisterhood of St. John the Baptist in 1892. She died of pneumonia in 1897 and is memorialized in a window at the rear of Old Grace Church.

Chapter 5

NEW SETTLERS, NEW FEATURES AFTER 1870

FARMING DISTRICT

Massapequa's farming district developed after the Civil War, independently of Jones or Floyd-Jones influence. Most farming residents came from one of the several states that made up what became a united Germany and settled in what was known then as South Oyster Bay. They probably left the German states because of the ongoing local wars between Prussia and the smaller German states that led to a unified Germany in 1871. The newly arrived settlers farmed in the area between Jerusalem Avenue and Boundary Avenue east and west of Hicksville Road. Most farmers were German, but there was an Italian family (Mandra), an eastern European family (Mysliwiecs) and even a Chinese family, whose laborers wore large straw hats and long pants.[31]

Massapequa's farmers sold a wide variety of produce: strawberries, potatoes, beans, tomatoes, carrots, rhubarb, corn, apples and more. Some families grew asters and dahlias for the New York City flower market, and there was at least one poultry farm, selling eggs and chickens. There was also a butcher in the area. Produce was sold locally, to the Jones and Floyd-Jones estates as well as to other residents of the sparsely settled area, or trucked either to the Westbury auction market or directly into New York City. One attraction for farm families was the South Side Railroad, today's Long Island Rail Road Babylon branch, completed in 1867.

Most farms were five to ten acres, but the Meyer farm near North Suffolk Avenue was larger than thirty acres. The farmers recruited youngsters to help with the planting and harvesting, with the result that farm families developed a strong sense of community, held regular social events and attended Grace Church on Merrick Road, at that time the only church in the Massapequas. Their presence strained the church's capacity. It was, after all, built in 1844 as a family church for the Floyd-Jones family and could accommodate no more than about one hundred people. By the late 1800s, it had become too small for the local population. The only church in the vicinity needed to be modernized, or the church leadership needed to find another solution.

In 1894, Reverend William Wiley, newly installed head of Grace Church, preached a sermon entitled "Other Sheep I Have that Are Not of This Fold." He used it as a rallying cry to build a separate church for the farming district. His efforts succeeded, as Grace Church's wardens decided to build a local chapel to provide a worship space for the farm community. The result was St. Christopher's Chapel, completed in 1899 on Hicksville Road just north of Bayberry Lane. It became the center of social and religious activity for local farmers for half a century and for subsequent residents until the late 1970s. The chapel reflected a significant trend within the American Episcopal Church, whose leaders moved to create separate congregations to minister to the needs of individuals. As the United States industrialized and urbanized, and people migrated from European and Asian countries, church leaders encouraged the creation of worship sites that would attract specific groups, such as the farming community in Northwest Massapequa.

Reverend Wiley's son Ralph wrote a very insightful book entitled *Preacher's Son* about life in the Massapequas at the turn of the twentieth century. He was born in 1893 and describes the Massapequas as "a land of country estates, nearly all owned by one family." He and his friends went hunting, fishing and boating on South Oyster Bay and had very few encumbrances in the way of roads, traffic, clusters of houses or stores. During the school year, he attended the one-room schoolhouse located on today's Park Boulevard and later Amityville High School. He mentioned that he missed several of his friends, who lived on the estates and returned to New York City as the weather cooled. For some Floyd-Joneses, then, South Oyster Bay was still a place for summer vacationing.

Old Grace Church was run in a very direct and forceful way by Reverend Wiley. He did not have the services of a vestry of active members or

St. Christopher's chapel. *Courtesy of the Historical Society of the Massapequas.*

committees or clubs such as women's groups, and when the New Year began, he reminded the congregation that the church would need a specific sum for its yearly expenses and that everybody was expected to contribute to the budget the following Sunday. For a brief period, he ministered to Seaford residents by holding services in a tavern on Merrick Road, but that practice ended when George Stanton Floyd-Jones and his sisters started St.

Michael and All Angels Church on Jackson Avenue. Wiley and Floyd-Jones became close friends, despite George's conversion to Roman Catholicism after marrying his wife, Anita.

QUEENS LAND AND TITLE COMPANY

Allen and George Haight created the Queens Land and Title Company in the 1890s and were looking for sites to build what they expected would become a new city of fifteen thousand residents in the Massapequas. They had bought three thousand acres from the Jones and Floyd-Jones families on either side of Hicksville Road, from the Farm District to Merrick Road. They advertised their project in a valuable photo book entitled *Seeing Massapequa by Pictures*, which is available in the Floyd-Jones Library. The company ran free trains every Sunday and built several hundred houses, but it lacked the capital to complete its ambitious project. It did, however, create a district of unique houses that stand today.

In about 1908, the Haights were approached by leaders of the National Fire Proofing Company, which had built several skyscrapers in Manhattan using hollow clay tile blocks. City builders preferred to use steel, which was cheaper and more versatile, especially in taller buildings. The company worked with the Haights to select a plot south of the railroad and east of Hicksville Road, with a plan to build forty fireproof houses. The Haights were only able to build twelve, however, before they became unable to meet their mortgage payments and their property was foreclosed. Ten of the twelve houses still stand, and one was recently given landmark status because of its construction and appearance.[32]

Queens Land and Title Company's efforts provided some development of the western part of the Massapequas, but not the widespread changes it projected. Photos of the area in the 1920s and 1930s show isolated houses with extensive open spaces on either side of Hicksville Road. Youngsters who lived there went to the Plainedge School, which was closer than the Massapequa School, opened in 1925 and the only school in the Massapequas until the late 1940s. Catholic students could attend St. William the Abbot School in Seaford or St. Martin of Tours School in Amityville. There was no Catholic school in the Massapequas until St. Rose of Lima School opened in 1956. A photo collection, given to the historical society by a former resident whose grandparents bought a house

Fireproof house on Ocean Avenue. *Author's collection.*

on Chicago Avenue in 1922, documents the relatively sparse settlement of northwest Massapequa before World War II.

The Massapequas' population remained very low because of the presence of the large Jones and Floyd-Jones estates. There were 450 grammar school students and 150 high school students in 1940. The latter attended high school either in Amityville or Baldwin after graduating from the Massapequa School. It was originally built to hold 100 students, but the number increased steadily in the 1920s and 1930s, forcing several expansions. Changes were coming, as the older estates disappeared and newer communities such as Massapequa Park enticed New York City dwellers to move to "the country."

FIRE AND WATER

The slow but steady growth of Massapequa's population prompted several residents to create a fire department in order to provide an organized method of combating fires throughout the area. Several meetings of a group of ten volunteers led to the incorporation of the Massapequa Fire Department in 1910. The members raised money among themselves and their neighbors to buy a fire truck that was pulled by horses borrowed from local farmers to respond to alarms. A Model T truck was bought in 1920, the first motorized fire truck. About the same time, a two-story red brick building was built on Grand Avenue as the first firehouse. That building remains today as the headquarters of the Massapequa Water District.

The steady population increases of the '20s and '30s, spurred by Queens Land and Title Company's construction of many houses along Hicksville Road, led to the construction of a large firehouse on Hicksville Road just north of Sunrise Highway in 1940. Explosive growth in Massapequa Park brought about the Park District Firehouse on Front Street in 1952, and developments along Merrick Road and south toward South Oyster Bay prompted construction of the East End House on Merrick Road and East Shore Drive in 1962, replacing a smaller garage at the site. These three houses serve as headquarters for 280 volunteers who respond to more than 2,500 calls each year.

Water also became an issue in the 1920s, not only for firefighting but for home usage as well. There were very few water pipes in the area, and residents began to question the Town of Oyster Bay about creating an area-wide distribution system. A reservoir existed from 1890, dug out north of the railroad tracks and west of Park Boulevard, but it, and several others along the south shore, were built by New York City to serve its water needs. The town created a Water District in 1930 and negotiated with New York City to take control of the reservoir. The original customer base in 1930 was 672 residents living at 184 sites. Because of strong opposition in the late 1920s from George Stanton Floyd-Jones, who owned Sewan, and Louise Floyd-Jones Thorn, who owned Little Unqua (both of whom could pump their own water), the southeastern part of the Massapequas was not incorporated in the Water District and is today served by New York American Water. Further, the area north of Jerusalem Avenue is serviced by the Farmingdale Water District, using lines laid originally in the 1920s.[33]

Parenthetically, the Massapequas have never had their own police department. Police services are provided by Nassau County and the State of New York.

HOTELS

A unique feature of the Massapequas was the existence of fifteen hotels, built at various times in the late nineteenth century. Massapequa gained a reputation as a convenient vacation retreat close to New York City, which was undergoing rapid population growth from Irish, Italian and Jewish immigrants. The best-known hotel was Massapequa Hotel, built in 1888 on Ocean Avenue south of Merrick Road. The hotel was owned by William Snedeker. It had three hundred rooms and was equipped with a dining room, a dance hall, a drawing room and larger than normal beds. It also had a billiard parlor and a bowling alley. There was a wraparound porch where guests could sit and enjoy the fresh air.

Outdoor recreation activities included golfing at a course laid out to the west of the building; bathing at a beach with a pavilion, named Billy's Beach after the owner's son; boating; cycling; and opportunities to hunt in the surrounding woods or to fish in Massapequa Lake, just to the north. There were also five cottages that could be used for overflow customers or rented for the summer season. The cottages and the hotel had electricity, indoor plumbing and hot and cold water, luxuries for the time. Another appeal to New Yorkers was its comparative closeness. One advertisement

Massapequa Hotel. *Courtesy of the Historical Society of the Massapequas.*

described it as "delightfully situated at Massapequa...28 miles from Greater New York...reached by express trains from Long Island City and Flatbush Avenue stations in forty minutes."[34]

The hotel was very popular for several years, with daily rates from three dollars per room or twelve dollars per week. A registry kept by the Historical Society of the Massapequas showed that most of the guests were from Brooklyn and New York City, although there are entries for guests from Sleepy Hollow, Philadelphia, New Orleans, Tacoma, Mexico City and Paris. Many New Yorkers were members of bicycle clubs, with the Brooklyn Bicycle Club securing rooms for its members on several occasions. Bicycling was a very popular sport around the turn of the century, so it's easy to envision legions of bicyclers (wheelmen, as they were commonly known, even though there were many female bicyclists) traveling along South Oyster Bay Road (Merrick Road) during the good weather.

The hotel began to lose business in the early 1900s for reasons that are not entirely clear. Snedeker closed the building in 1914 and sold off its fixtures. Several walls and a section of the building were used to construct Panchard's Hotel on Merrick Road, which lasted until the early 1950s. The cottages still stand along Ocean Avenue, with a large "S" for Snedeker still affixed to the front of one. The hotel is a shining example of the decidedly rural character of the Massapequas well into the twentieth century. The historical society has erected a marker commemorating the building at the entrance to the Massapequa Preserve on Merrick Road and Ocean Avenue.

Woodcastle Hotel was another building that served guests from New York City. It was built in 1870 by Clara and Louis Dessart, who were among the several dozen Alsatian residents who settled in the area around what later became Front Street in Massapequa Park in the late 1800s. The area took on a Germanic character, with the Apollo Beer Garden just west of the hotel. The building was popular until the early 1900s but closed before World War I. Many of the residents with German backgrounds left the area after the war, and the area lost its Germanic character. It fell victim to the population explosion after World War II and was torn down by the Village of Massapequa Park and replaced by the Park Firehouse in 1952. A stately mulberry tree planted before 1900 stands just east of the firehouse on Front Street today.

A few residents remain as the descendants of the Dessarts, among them Lillian Bryson, whose parents, Charlotte and Frank Rumfield, lived in the hotel and sold it to the fire department. Lillian's mother attended the one-room schoolhouse on Wurttemberg Road, later Park Boulevard, so her roots, and those of her children and grandchildren, go very deep in the Massapequas.

The Schaefer Homestead was another residence built by Germanic settlers around 1900 a few blocks west of Woodcastle Hotel. It was occupied by the family for several decades but was sold to the Village of Massapequa Park in the 1930s. The village used it as its business hall, but the building also fell victim to the population expansion and was torn down and replaced by a new and larger Village Hall, completed in 1966, which stands today.

ACTORS AND ACTRESSES

Another unique development in the early 1900s was the creation of an informal theater district. Before the internet, television and radio, and at the very beginnings of motion pictures, New Yorkers flocked to the theater for live productions. One of the best-known entertainers of the time was Fred Stone, who appeared in many musical comedies. Among the most popular were *Tip Top*, *Chin Chin* and *The Red Mill*. Stone appeared with his wife and children and billed them as the "Rolling Stones." In 1915, aware of Massapequa's reputation as a place for rural rest and relaxation, he bought a piece of property in the eastern part, south of Merrick Road, where Stone Boulevard, Clocks Boulevard and County Line Road are located today. It was convenient to his house in Forest Hills and the Broadway theaters. He built a large yellow house on Narraskatuck Creek; laid out a polo field, riding track and park; and built two cabins to entertain guests and named it Chin Chin Ranch.

Among those who visited were Tom Mix, Annie Oakley, Douglas Fairbanks Sr., Leo Carillo, Rex Beach, Irene and Vernon Castle and Will Rogers. Rogers was so impressed with the area that he rented a house across the street from Stone's and lived there for many years. The Duke of Windsor, later King George VI, also visited to play polo.

Will Rogers suffered an unexpected injury that ironically enhanced his career. He dove off the back of Stone's dock into Narraskatuck Creek and injured himself because the water was shallower than he expected. He damaged his right shoulder and had to alter his vaudeville career, so he took to twirling his rope with his left hand and telling stories, making him more popular than he had been.

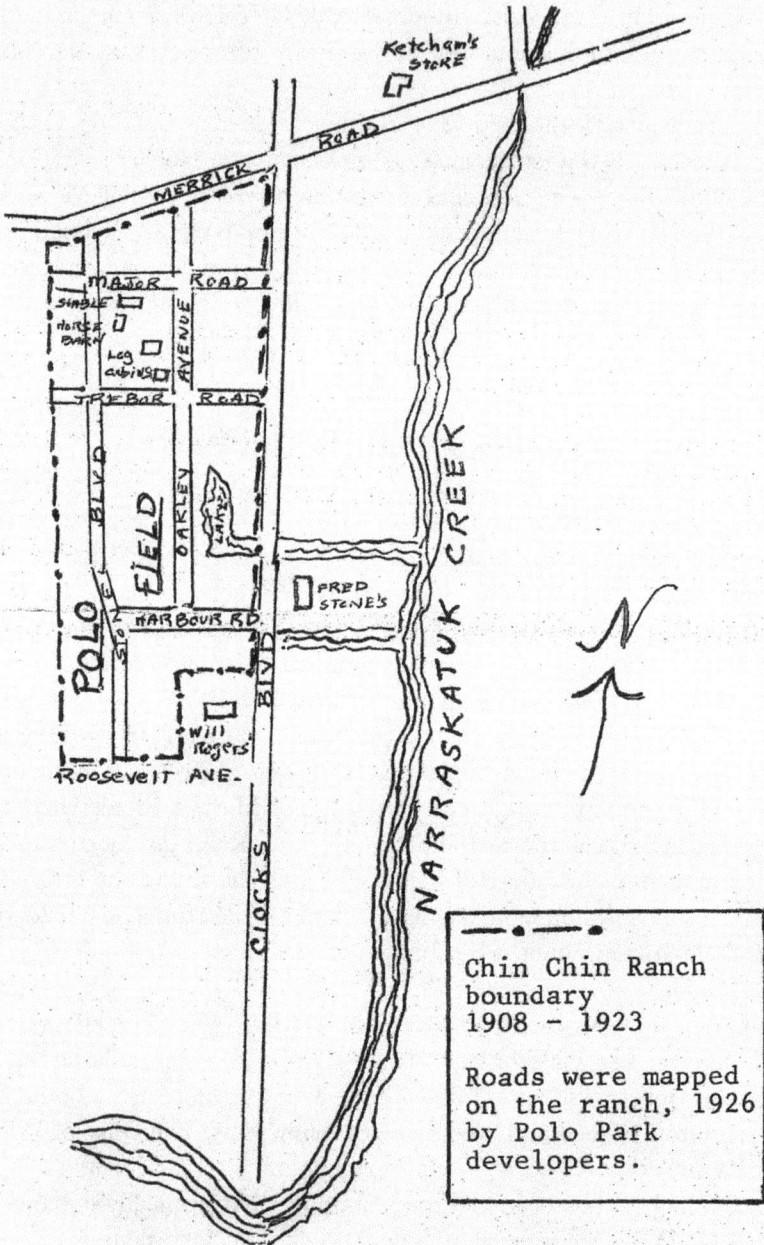

Chin Chin Ranch Grounds. *Courtesy of the Historical Society of the Massapequas.*

Stone sold his house and the ranch in 1925 and spent more time in Hollywood, appearing in many motion pictures. The two cabins were rented by their owners for many years but deteriorated in the 1960s and 1970s as houses were built around them. In 1985, the local Kiwanis Organization disassembled the larger of the two cabins (the smaller building could not be saved), numbered each piece and moved them to John Burns Park, where it was rebuilt and stands today at the southeast corner, used by Boy Scouts and as a town storage area. It remains as an out-of-the-way but valuable reminder of Massapequa's unique history. This effort was completed in 1986, the same year the historical society moved the Floyd-Jones servants' cottage, two examples of a growing awareness of the necessity to save artifacts of local history.

LONG ISLAND RAIL ROAD

The Long Island Rail Road was a major contributor to the changes in the Massapequas after 1870. The first line was completed in 1844 and ran through the center of the island. After the Civil War, investors felt that there was money to be made in creating a line connecting the several towns that existed along the south shore. Accordingly, they pooled their money and created the South Side Railway, completing the line from Jamaica to Babylon in October 1867. Running time was one hour and fifteen minutes, and the fare from Jamaica to Babylon was $0.85. The line provided easy access to New York City and Brooklyn (then a separate city) for the farmers in North Massapequa, as well as for Floyd-Jones family members traveling to and from their homes in Lower Manhattan. One of the first mortgage holders was David Richard Floyd-Jones ($750,000). Elbert Floyd-Jones acquired a $500,000 mortgage in 1871 that financed construction of a second track.

In 1886, a modest wooden station was built for South Oyster Bay but was replaced in 1890 with money provided by George Stanton Floyd-Jones, who felt his family's location deserved a large and ornate station. He also convinced the line's owners at the time to rename the station "Massapequa," a name that was becoming common to identify the area. His friendship with Austin Corbin, president of the Long Island Rail Road, which had bought the South Side line in 1876, facilitated these developments. The railroad made it easier for visitors from New York

City to travel and stay at one of the many hotels that were built in the Massapequa "countryside."[35] It also became a critical link for local farmers who wanted to sell their flowers, vegetables and more in the Westbury market—or in New York City after 1910, when a tunnel was built under the East River and track was laid to Penn Station.

Chapter 6

GROWTH BETWEEN THE WARS

EDUCATION

The Massapequas had a one-room schoolhouse for many years, beginning in the 1840s. It was located along Merrick Road east of Massapequa Manor. The original building burned in 1852 and was soon rebuilt. In the late 1870s, it was moved to Schoolhouse Road (later Park Boulevard) because the students were distracted by the horse races held at a nearby track. A second room was added in 1910 to accommodate the increase of students because of the population growth related to the farming district and Queens Land and Title houses along Hicksville Road. There were twenty students, as seen in a 1910 photo, and four teachers taught the different class levels. Attendance increased after a 1913 New York State law that mandated 180 days of instruction for all students ages six to sixteen.

The influence of the Floyd-Jones family can be seen clearly regarding the school. The first trustee was Elbert Floyd-Jones, from 1867 to 1890. He was succeeded by George Stanton Floyd-Jones from 1891 to 1906. Edward H. Floyd-Jones served from 1907 to 1924, at which time a three-person board was created.

By 1925, a new school was clearly needed, as the population continued to grow. The Massapequa Board of Trade and the Massapequa Civic Association supported the school leadership and the Town of Oyster Bay in its request to the State Education Department. Spurred on by

School on Schoolhouse Road in 1914. *Courtesy of Delancey Floyd-Jones Free Library.*

discussions with town officials, the Department of Education approved creation of School District 23, to be overseen by a board of trustees. In the first board, elected in 1925, Edward H. Floyd-Jones was the chairman. Board members agreed about the need for a modern school and authorized construction of a five-room brick building, designed by a local architect, at a cost of $92,000, which would include plumbing, heating, a phone system, furniture and landscaping around the building. One of the bones of contention was the location, with some members favoring a site near the LIRR tracks. Financial considerations prevailed, however, and the cheaper current location was chosen despite it being a low area, north of Merrick Road and west of Massapequa Lake, with a stream running underneath. This prevented the trustees from building a basement, so that the original school remained at ground level until the late 1940s, when a basement was added as part of a major overhaul to accommodate the growing population.

Massapequa's first "modern" school, the five-room Massapequa School, was built of brick and could accommodate eighty students. There were six teachers and a principal. As the school population grew, Raymond Lockhart was named principal, the first male teacher and male principal in the area's history. The original enrollment of eighty-one students in 1925 grew to two hundred by the beginning of World War II, steady growth that required physical expansion. Four additional classrooms were added in 1931, including one that was used exclusively for industrial arts, taught by Mr. Lockhart. He was also the eighth-grade teacher and principal in the 1930–31 school year.

The Massapequa School remained cramped through the 1930s, with a small kitchen under the stage and lunches lifted up to the auditorium level. There was a small faculty room and an even smaller office, which was occupied by Mary Lockhart, the principal's wife, who came in one day each week to provide clerical service. Marjorie Post also worked there as a secretary.

Several incidents show how different the environment was then. During lunchtime, boys would often walk east toward Massapequa Lake to visit with a cow that belonged to a local farmer. Some would also steal apples from the trees behind a house overlooking the lake. Other incidents included students spending lunchtime resting under a large chestnut tree to the south of the school, eating the chestnuts as snacks. One teacher remembers taking her class out of the building and being urged by pheasant hunters to bring them back inside for their safety. On a few occasions, students were asked to collect sacs of tent caterpillar eggs to combat their attacks on trees. One year, the PTA offered a five-dollar reward to the student who brought in the most sacs.

There was also a problem with the stream that ran under the building and the playground. After heavy rains, children were required to walk on planks put over the wet areas, which led to mud being tracked into the building. Children waited eagerly for the end of school on very cold winter days, so they could skate on nearby Massapequa Lake.[36]

Massapequa Park

The area that became Massapequa Park was sparsely settled by 1918. Many of the German residents who had settled near Front Street moved after World War I because of anti-German sentiment. Wurttemberg Road, in fact, was renamed Schoolhouse Road and later Park Boulevard. Sears Roebuck, which sold more than seventy thousand prefabricated Modern Homes nationwide from 1908 to 1942, offered to provide homes in the area for those who wished to build their own or hire contractors and skilled craftspeople to build them. Several dozen homes were built in Massapequa Park, most in the Hollywood Gardens area north of the railroad tracks and along Grand Boulevard, Pacific Street and Charles Avenue. Costs began at $499 for the pre-cut material for a standard four-room house with one bath on one floor ("The Hudson"). Prices increased depending on size and style, as well as whether the buyer wished to use outside services, as well as the type of heating desired. Sears called these houses "Honor Built" and guaranteed the size and fit of all material. The most expensive was "The Glen Falls," priced at $4,909, featuring two floors, four bedrooms and two full baths. Most in Massapequa Park are still standing today.[37]

Matthew Brady, Frank Cryan and Peter Colleran (often abbreviated as BCC) had more ambitious plans. They were Irish real estate agents who attracted many hundreds of New Yorkers with their promise of affordable houses on spacious sites near to New York City by train or plane. In order to have maximum control of their enterprise, they convinced the New York State legislature to create the Village of Massapequa Park. The

Brady, Cryan and Colleran. *Courtesy of the Historical Society of the Massapequas.*

vote approving creation of the village was seventy-nine to thirty-nine, underscoring how sparsely populated the area was in 1930. The village began operations in 1931 and was controlled by BCC, acting independently of the Town of Oyster Bay.

The location was suggested by their friend and fellow Irishman Governor Al Smith, who had heard that Robert Moses planned to build a road from the new Southern State Parkway to Jones Beach through the area. BCC bought a one-and-a-half-mile-wide stretch of property from the Southern State parkway down to Merrick Road. Unfortunately for them, the road was completed farther west and became Wantagh Parkway, but BCC continued to promote their new town with great initial success. The earliest houses were red brick structures built south of Sunrise Highway—along Glengariff Road, Tyrconnell Avenue and Avoca Avenue—and priced at $8,000.

FITZMAURICE FLYING FIELD

When BCC planned out Massapequa Park, they decided to include a flying field at its center. They hoped that it would attract homebuyers who owned small planes and would welcome the opportunity to keep their planes near their homes, either to commute to work or for pleasure.

One of the best-known early female aviators was Elinor Smith, born in Freeport and attracted to flying by her father, Tom. She became famous for setting altitude, distance and endurance records and for being the only flier to fly under all four East River bridges, accomplishing the feat in 1927 when she was only sixteen years old. She retired from flying when she had children but returned to aviation in later life. She was featured in Massapequa Park's 1976 bicentennial parade because of her connection with Fitzmaurice Field.

BCC contacted her through her father, Tom, and invited both of them to look for a suitable spot for an airfield. Smith selected the area in the very middle of what became Massapequa Park, equidistant from the Southern State Parkway and Sunrise Highway, both of which were being completed through the Massapequas, and between the Massapequa Preserve and the Suffolk County line. The site, with an 1,800-foot runway, the shortest on Long Island, remained isolated from houses until after World War II.

Charles Lindbergh made world history by flying solo across the Atlantic in May 1927. One year later, three men flew the more difficult east–west route, from Ireland to Newfoundland. They were Hermann Köhl,

Massapequa Park showing Fitzmaurice Field, 1938. *Courtesy of the Incorporated Village of Massapequa Park.*

Baron Ehrenfried von Hünefeld and Colonel James Fitzmaurice, flying in a Junkers plane named *The Bremen*. The latter achieved further fame by having his name attached to the airport built in 1929 in what later became Massapequa Park.

Colonel Fitzmaurice, who was commandant of the Irish National Army Air Service, and his two companions left Dublin in *The Bremen* on April 12, 1928, and landed on Greenly Island in Labrador the next day. Despite their failure to reach New York City, they were hailed as heroes by Canadian and American newspapers. They were awarded the Distinguished Flying Cross by President Calvin Coolidge and were honored with a ticker-tape parade.[38] Baron Gottfried von Hünefeld and Hermann Köhl have streets named after them in the area where the airfield was located. Lindbergh Street is nearby, as is Smith Street, which was named after Elinor Smith and was the southern border of Fitzmaurice Field.

Brady Cryan and Colleran saw value in having Fitzmaurice give his name to the airfield. It opened to great fanfare in May 1929 with a crowd estimated at fifty thousand people. Many famous aviators attended, including Clarence Chamberlain, Bert Acosta, Elinor Smith and Viola Gentry. BCC created an Irish Aero Club and named Tom Murphy to manage the airfield. He eventually passed on the field to his son Tom, deepening the Irish connection the real estate firm had established as the bedrock for Massapequa Park. The field was popular with some residents but never became as busy as BCC had planned. The Great Depression, starting with the October 1929 stock market crash, shook the new village to its foundations, and BCC's questionable business practices affected the growth of Massapequa Park.

At the height of their activities, BCC employed 650 real estate agents, sending them to Irish neighborhoods in New York City, specifically

Sunnyside and Woodside in Queens and most of the Bronx north of Tremont Avenue. The enticements were inexpensive land and houses (between $7,950 and $8,950), with open spaces and easy access to New York City. They reserved trains to bring prospective buyers out to the area, bussed them to specific sites north and south of newly completed Sunrise Highway and provided corned beef dinners to all who visited. In fact, their office on Sunrise Highway and Park Boulevard became commonly known as the "corned beef and cabbage building."

Records show that homes worth $131,000 were sold on BCC's opening day, November 6, 1927. In one day in May 1929, 5,621 people visited what became Massapequa Park, riding on trains provided by BCC. On some Sundays, two trains were needed to accommodate customers. One result of this activity was that the Long Island Railroad agreed to open a new station at Park Boulevard in Massapequa Park, its first in twenty-five years. It was completed in October 1933, replacing a whistle stop built by the Floyd-Jones family just west of Unqua Road.

The Great Depression bankrupted many of the people who had put down money for homes. BCC kept payments made by customers but delayed

Tom Murphy's plane at Fitzmaurice Field. *Courtesy of the Incorporated Village of Massapequa Park.*

building homes and reneged on running water or sewer pipes or power lines to the sites that were purchased. Several buyers alleged that their contracts were written in such a way that BCC could void them on flimsy pretexts and could keep their money. After several lawsuits, their real estate licenses were revoked in October 1932, with one appellate opinion upholding a judgment for a female plaintiff, citing "the signing of the contract in blank, and the unbusinesslike transfer in blank of her bank account in making payments for the lots, all of which tend to show that she was easily misled by the assurances and allurements held out to her by the appellant's salesman."[39]

Peter Colleran was indicted for fraud but agreed to resign as mayor of Massapequa Park rather than face jail time. Frank Cryan was convicted but agreed to leave the area and avoided jail time also. Michael Brady seemed to escape unscathed. He had remained in New York City, handling the real estate transactions as well as the firm's legal details. He became Massapequa Park's village justice and held that post until 1964. Many of the people who

Massapequa Park train station in the 1930s. *Courtesy of the Incorporated Village of Massapequa Park.*

had bought lots never received refunds, but many others had houses built that became the nucleus of Massapequa Park, settling in streets north and south of Sunrise Highway and east and west of Park Boulevard.

Brady Park, next to the Massapequa Reservoir, is named after Frank Brady, and Colleran Park, at the foot of Skylark Road and Whitewood Drive, is named after Peter Colleran. Frank Cryan does not have a memorial.

The fate of Fitzmaurice Field is starkly reflective of the Massapequas' pre- and postwar development. Several homeowners kept their planes there, but the surrounding area never developed to the point that it became a crowded airfield. Hangars were built at the north end, and the planes kept there were used as trainers for young pilots. Tom Murphy Jr. became a licensed instructor and taught hundreds of youngsters the basics of aviation. Flying was curtailed during World War II, as fuel and parts became diverted to the war effort. After 1945, Tom Tyler operated a stunt flying school, and the field became a center for skywriters, who had a large captive audience at nearby Jones Beach. It was also used to store old planes and repair parts.

FOX FRANKEL

William Fox was a wealthy film magnate in the 1920s. He was looking for a place to invest his immense wealth and saw an opportunity in the Massapequas. With his partner Joseph Frankel, he built several dozen Spanish-style houses in Biltmore Shores as well as in Merrick Gables, several miles west. His houses featured stucco walls, stained-glass windows, red tile roofs and wrought-iron fences. He also dug out a swimming area known as Fox Lagoon, which was the deepest water in the Massapequas at 125 feet. Unfortunately, the two men suffered disastrously as a result of the stock market crash in 1929 and sold their properties to Harmon National Bank.

Many other properties were affected by the Great Depression. In 1933, a large auction was held of property "Adjacent to Massapequa Railroad Station," with auctioneer James R. Murphy aiming to sell 190 lots. He touted the advantages of Massapequa as a developing area, with houses being built throughout the area. He recalled the post-1918 era, when there was a housing shortage because of the war, and urged prospective bidders to take advantages of the rock-bottom prices that property owners were willing to take. Residential lots were offered for five dollars per month and business lots for ten dollars per month.

Biltmore Shores Administrative Building

WILLIAM FOX

JOSEPH FRANKEL.

The Men
Behind
Biltmore Shores

Left: William Fox
and Joseph Frankel.
*Courtesy of the
Historical Society of the
Massapequas.*

Below: Fox Frankel's
Spanish-style house.
Author's collection.

HARBOUR GREEN

Harbour Green was unusual for its development in the 1930s. It was located on Merrick Road, east of what was by then the Wagon Wheel Restaurant and directly across from Grace Church. The Fox Frankel endeavor had failed because of the 1929 stock market crash, and Harmon National Bank had bought several hundred acres from Merrick Road down to the bay. Massapequa's population numbered about one thousand residents, so there was abundant land available. The depression had made it difficult, however, for people to buy houses or even keep the houses they owned.

The bank's leaders guessed that buyers would be interested in larger pieces of property than usual and would be satisfied with a smaller house if it could be set in a rural area, so they set out to divide the area into one-hundred-foot-square lots and design small houses without cellars or porches, with white siding, black roofs and black or green shutters. They chose Belgian paving blocks instead of sidewalks, retaining the rural appearance. Their slogan became "The Minimum House on the Maximum Plot." They were careful to leave existing trees where they stood, laying out streets that protected the wild cherry, pepperidge, maple, cedar and hemlock trees that graced the area. They acted as their own contractor, charged 50 percent down and gave long-term mortgages for the remainder.

The development was named Harbour Green, and the first house was built in the summer of 1931. Mr. and Mrs. George Pearson were the first residents. Their house was on Bay Drive and Hampton Boulevard, and their only neighbors were the rector of Grace Church, whose house fronted on Merrick Road; Frank Avignone; and William Wiley Jr., who had built houses on Central Avenue in the 1920s. There were no paved roads for several years, and the Town of Oyster Bay did not provide snow plowing or leaf collection services until after 1945. Residents enjoyed the country look and feel of Harbor Green, and it was featured in a 1936 *LIFE* magazine article as an example of unique homebuilding. By 1941, Harmon National Bank had contracted out the home building, extending the community down to Dartmouth Road. World War II ended this and almost all construction in the Massapequas.[40]

Eugene Bryson, a longtime member of the historical society and warden of Grace Church, reminisced in 1989 about accompanying his father, who was digging foundations on Bay Drive in 1937 for the expansion of Harbour Green. The workers found bones and uncovered

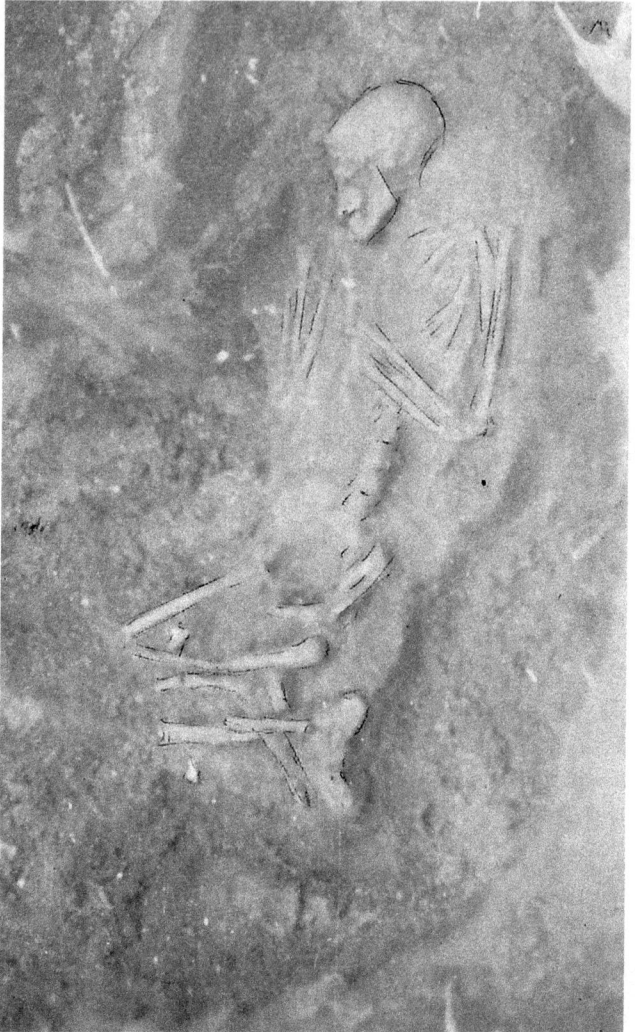

Skeleton uncovered on Bay Drive in 1937. *Courtesy of the Historical Society of the Massapequas.*

a human skeleton. Work stopped while archaeologists were consulted. They identified the bones as Native American, took pictures and then removed them. One year later, an extensive dig was made of the wider area, and many other native remains were found, as well as remnants of a fort and path to an apparent camp. The remains were donated to the American Museum of Natural History. The site was later recognized by a sign erected by the Town of Oyster Bay.

FRANK BUCK ZOO

The Frank Buck Zoo was another unique site developed between the wars. Frank Buck was an enormously famous big game hunter, known for his "bring 'em back alive" approach, where he would capture African animals and bring them to the United States to exhibit them. After earning huge fame at the 1932 Chicago World's Fair, he constructed a zoo in eastern Massapequa, just south of the newly created Sunrise Highway. The zoo featured large cats, giraffes, elephants, reptiles, zebras and antelopes, the latter kept in a five-acre "African veldt" at the back of the property. The zoo also featured a seventy-five-foot-high Monkey Mountain, where several hundred monkeys would play, to the delight of adults and children alike. The zoo was enormously popular through the '30s, attracting up to twenty-five thousand visitors on summer weekends. It also attracted national attention in 1934, when 150 monkeys escaped from Monkey Mountain over an unguarded walkway. All the monkeys were eventually returned. One longtime resident remembers feeding a monkey who had jumped onto her porch a banana until the keepers came.

Buck lost interest in the zoo in the early 1940s, and the war, with its rationing restrictions, made it difficult to feed and care for the animals. Gasoline rationing also made travel to such an attraction very inconvenient. His partners leased the property to the Concord Manufacturing Company, which reprocessed spent cartridges into bullets and sold them to police forces and military training camps, to be used by recruits. Buck died in 1950.

Frank Buck Zoo.
Courtesy of the Historical Society of the Massapequas.

After the war, the Grimaldi family purchased six acres at the front of the property and ran the Massapequa Zoo until 1965, featuring small animals and children's rides. The zoo closed in 1965, and the property is today a shopping center.

Panchard's

Several sections of the Massapequa Hotel were moved in 1914 to a site on Hicksville and Merrick Roads (site of the former Van De Water Hotel) and were used to build Panchard's Hotel. In addition to providing rooms, it also had a ballroom that attracted many famous entertainers in the 1920s and 1930s—the acts were transmitted over radio, which became common by the early 1930s. Kate Smith was one of the headliners who appeared there. The building burned in 1952 and became a farmers' market. The site is occupied today by a gas station and several storefronts. Ivan Jerome was the owner.

Mr. Jerome was well known in the community for attracting famous entertainers. He was also lauded for having developed in the early '20s a method by which helicopters could hover in the air, as well as for having perfected the Norden bombsight, used by almost all U.S. planes in World War II. Unfortunately, he had an unsavory side, being arrested for having lured many teenage girls to his hotel and house in Southampton for sex orgies and other forms of abuse. He was arrested and charged in 1955 and became known as the "Monster of Massapequa." While out on bail, he escaped and was never found. Longtime residents often nod ruefully when the name Panchard's is mentioned.

By 1941, the Massapequas still featured Floyd-Jones mansions on Merrick Road but also contained developments that were only partially complete: Queens Land and Title in the northwest, fireproof houses south of Sunrise Highway, Sears houses and Brady Cryan and Colleran houses in Massapequa Park, as well as Spanish-style Fox Frankel houses and Harbour Green dwellings south of Merrick Road. The area was still minimally developed compared to Seaford, Amityville and other nearby Nassau County communities. The expansion would have to wait until the end of the war.

Panchard's Restaurant. *Courtesy of the Historical Society of the Massapequas.*

WORLD WAR II

Most construction stopped during World War II, as metal, wood and other materials were needed for the war effort. There was very little gasoline available, so most people sold their cars. Ration books were provided to local citizens, who could buy scarce commodities according to specific schedules. To aid the war effort, corn was grown in the field that later became John Burns Park, and residents planted vegetables and fruit in Liberty Gardens, vacant plots near their homes.

Chapter 7

POSTWAR DEVELOPMENT

Two sets of numbers hint at the explosive growth of the Massapequas after World War II. The population of Massapequa Park in 1950 was 2,334; in 1958, it was 17,729. The population of the Massapequas without Massapequa Park was 3,500 in 1940 and 40,000 in 1960.[41]

HOUSING

The population of the Massapequas soared after 1945, as returning servicemen looked for homes for their families that would provide open space and less crowded conditions than existed in New York City. Most of those who relocated came from Brooklyn and western Queens (e.g., Astoria and Long Island City), while eastern Queens (e.g., Bayside, Fresh Meadows, Floral Park) became populated and took on some of the trappings of suburbia. The overall aim was to escape from an urban environment, a sense that became common throughout the United States in the postwar period.

Several dozen real estate companies and home builders sprang up in the late '40s. This was a far cry from the individual activities of Queens Land and Title Company in the early 1900s and Brady Cryan and Colleran in the late '20s. Companies offered the same basic house, but each touted its own individuality and the superior quality of its construction. The Blakelock Company built several dozen houses for $7,000 in the late 1940s. A file of advertising brochures held by the historical society shows thirteen builders ready to construct houses with the most modern conveniences: large living rooms, two bathrooms, garages, basements, oil heat and baseboards instead of old-fashioned radiators.

Seven real estate offices were in various parts of the Massapequas—six were in Massapequa Park. Most of the model houses were located on Sunrise Highway or Hicksville Road. Prices ranged from $10,750 for a Hamilton Ranch to be built on Park Lane to $17,990 for a Cadillac House projected for the site of the former Corroon estate, originally Massapequa Manor. All offered easy financing, with veterans invited to buy with no cash down or with down payments that ranged between 5 percent and 10 percent of the prices. The average veteran's down payment was $695; the average standard down payment was $2,968 (circa 1952–53). The Massapequas were a perfect location for rapid development because there were relatively few houses standing after 1945. Older mansions owned by Jones or Floyd-Jones family members were showing their age by then and disappeared one after the other. Massapequa Manor, a prime location east of Massapequa Lake, was unoccupied for four years prior to its burning in November 1952. Cadillac Homes touted the location in its offering brochure, defending its relatively high price of $17,999 because of the superior location. The Peter Marshall Company built houses on North Queens Avenue for $13,000, with a basement for an additional $500.[42]

After 1945, Farm District land became ripe for development, and speculators pounced, offering the many small farmers attractive sums for their plots of land. For farmers who had spent their lives doing the hard, unrelenting and unpredictable work associated with living off the land, offers of cold cash proved irresistible, and the farms that had existed for almost a century disappeared within one generation after the war. The U.S. Agricultural Census provides striking confirmation of the change: the number of farms in Nassau County declined from 658 in 1945 to 83 in 1969 and the acreage under cultivation from 32,122 to 2,437.

Remnants of the farming district still exist in northwest Massapequa. Examples are St. Christopher's Chapel, since 1980 St. Gregory of Nyssa Church; Paddy's Loft Restaurant (the rear part was a barn); a barn on the east side of Hicksville Road south of the Southern State Parkway; and several farmhouses that have been remodeled. The farming district was memorialized by a historical marker raised in front of St. Gregory's Church in 1994 by the Historical Society of the Massapequas.

Arlyn Oaks development, 1952. *Courtesy of the Historical Society of the Massapequas.*

The first large postwar development was Arlyn Oaks, begun in 1950 and occupying land that was behind and east of the Unqua estate. It featured circular roads arranged concentrically and was located between Sunrise Highway and Merrick Road, both of which were developing as major shopping areas. Massapequa High School was completed shortly after to the west of the neighborhood. A contemporary image shows undeveloped land surrounding Arlyn Oaks.

WATER

The water needs of residents were met by the Massapequa Water District, created in 1931 to serve 184 customers. That number had exploded to 9,090 by 1955, requiring several new wells and miles of transmission lines. The district also took control of local water sources from the New York American Water Corporation, which had supplied water for several decades in the early 1900s. The number of connections reached 13,000 by 1985, and service was provided to 40,000 residents. Five wells were dug between 1954 and 1957, three along Ocean Avenue and two along Hicksville Road. One more was added on Sunrise Highway in 2003. There are now nine wells serving more than 35,000 residents. The enormous growth of the Water District in the postwar period simply underscores the unprecedented growth of the Massapequas during this time.[43]

SCHOOLS

The school system underwent enormous change inevitably, as new homeowners moved in with their young children or had children after they became Massapequans. The first "modern" school was the Massapequa School. Built in 1925 to replace a two-room "little red schoolhouse" that had stood on Park Boulevard for more than fifty years, it was constructed of brick and had four classrooms, a room for the principal and for the school administration, a kitchen and an auditorium that doubled as a cafeteria. It was expanded in 1930 and again in 1939, but that change was as nothing compared to what happened after 1945. That one school, for example, doubled in size in 1950 through the addition of a separate wing and creation of a basement.

Ironically, the original school did not have a basement because the ground was too wet because of the water level. As houses were built north of the school, leading up toward Sunrise Highway, water demands lowered the level and better construction techniques allowed District 23 to create a basement. The original building held 79 pupils in 1925 but 850 by 1948. Improvements to the first school, renamed Fairfield, helped students who lived in the area west of Massapequa Lake and north of Merrick Road. The rest of the district needed its own schools because it was bursting at the seams, with 2,000 enrolled students in 1950.

The first postwar school in the Massapequas was Ames (originally named Parkside), completed in 1950 for students north of Sunrise Highway. The school district leaders recognized the need to establish a comprehensive plan to accommodate the rapid growth of the student population. Much of the credit for the early years goes to Alfred Berner, a Queens banker who became active in school politics after 1945.

Alfred Berner had moved to the Massapequas in 1929, when Queens Land and Title Company was building houses near Hicksville Road. He became involved in the school system in 1945, first as a member of the board of education and then as president in 1950. He had a finance background and served as president of the First National City Bank branch in Queens Village. He was also active in the fire department as treasurer and as a vestryman at Grace Church. With his business background and "bottom line" approach to the educational system, he was instrumental in drawing up plans for the first several schools, overcoming the objections of taxpayers who were concerned about building costs by using wood instead of steel, which was more expensive and in short supply because of the Korean War, for construction. His influence was shorter than might be expected because he resigned from the board in 1954, citing business pressures. In fact, he had been ill for some time with a lung condition and died on July 7, 1956, after an operation. He was fifty-four years old.

The leadership gap was filled by Raymond Lockhart, who was intimately familiar with the school system. A gregarious and approachable leader, Lockhart had been the first male principal of the Massapequas (Massapequa School in 1930) and had overseen its expansion. In 1949, as district principal (the superintendent title came later), he proposed construction of a "new 15 classroom building to accommodate 450 elementary (kindergarten through sixth grade) pupils and located in the northern part of the district…at a cost of $850,000." The school was originally named Parkside but was renamed J. Lewis Ames School and expanded later for use as a potential high school.[44]

Ames School barely made a dent in the problem, however, because the district enrolled four thousand students for the 1952–53 school year. Students needed to be housed in temporary locations, and expedients were used: the Manor House, formerly George Stanton Floyd-Jones's estate known as Sewan, was used. It had become a Catholic school, but the school district was allowed to house public school students there. The Hicksville Road firehouse was used, as was Grace Church and the Mole Ford 10 car garage facility in Amityville, the latter for kindergartners.

The district had adopted a policy of being one school behind, the better to convince residents of the need to pay for new schools. Despite opening Unqua and East Lake schools in 1953, the district could not and would not get ahead of the problem. Both buildings were Class 3 construction, meaning they were built of wood, which was cheaper and allowed faster construction. Students remembered the smell of fresh polyurethane and how the fields were seas of mud because the district didn't have the luxury of time to grow grass. Despite this, many residents objected to the rise in taxes, and school board meetings were often raucous and divisive. Several budgets were, in fact, voted down.

Ironically, the large population that Brady Cryan and Colleran thought would be attracted by Fitzmaurice Flying Field in the 1930s led to its demise. Massapequa Park, as well as all of Nassau County, developed rapidly after World War II, and the proximity of houses to the airfield spurred concern among its new neighbors, who became fearful of planes taking off and landing so close to their backyards. An additional concern developed by 1950 as the rapid growth of the school system led the board of education to look for new sites. Fitzmaurice Flying Field was essentially a bare space ripe for development.

By 1952, District 23 was looking for any open spaces on which to build schools. Most space was gobbled up by builders, who were putting up houses at a frenetic pace. Fitzmaurice Field seemed an inviting target, so the board approached Tom Murphy, the owner, and offered him $600,000 for the property. Murphy was unenthusiastic but realized that he wasn't making much money as a flight trainer and could face the possibility of eminent domain proceedings, whereby New York State could take his property for a greater good (and schools were clearly the greater good). He therefore sold the Field for $600,000 in May 1953 and relocated to a field out in Coram, which, incidentally, lasted until 1980.

Murphy moved out his planes, equipment and hangars, leaving several empty buildings. A 4M Club held meetings at one of the old storage buildings until 1961. The rest of the property was used for public education. The board built Hawthorn School in 1954 at the southeast end of the field and McKenna Junior High School at the north end in 1958. Little do young soccer and baseball players know that hundreds of planes took off and landed on the fields where they play today.

New homeowners were settling all over the Massapequas, as can be seen by the locations of the new schools: Parkside (later Ames) on Broadway north of Sunrise Highway, Unqua on Unqua Road between Sunrise Highway and Merrick Road, East Lake in east central Massapequa Park and nearby Hawthorn, in the center of Massapequa Park. All were grammar schools, but it was clear that a high school was needed to accommodate graduates of Ames, which had become a junior high. Massapequa students had gone to Amityville High School or to Freeport or Baldwin High School for many decades, but the Amityville School District balked about continuing to admit a growing number of Massapequans. The message was that the time had come for Massapequa to build its own high school.

There were 7,500 students in District 23 by 1955, making a high school inevitable. Here again the influence of the Floyd-Jones family in Massapequa's

Top: Massapequa High School. *Courtesy of the Massapequa Public Library.*

Bottom: Berner High School. *Courtesy of the Massapequa Public Library.*

history was evident. George Stanton Floyd-Jones lived in Sewan and, upon his death, gave Sewan to the Dominican Sisters, who opened Queen of the Rosary Academy. It remained a Catholic school until 1952, when the district bought the property for the high school. Sewan was torn down, and a new building, rated Class 1 because of its steel construction, was built. The school held eighty classrooms on three floors, included a gym and library and was filled immediately, to the extent that there was no room for a large cafeteria. Students then as now could leave the building for lunch.

New buildings continued to open through the '50s, as the student population continued to expand. Carman's Road and Birch Lane were completed in 1956, known as sister schools because of their similar construction pattern. Birch Lane provides an excellent insight into the population growth: it was a few blocks south of Merrick Road, in an area that was at ground level and subject to flooding from South Oyster Bay. Builders who saw proximity to the water as a lucrative attraction began to fill in the area, using sand dredged from South Oyster Bay in a process called hydraulic fill. They laid out streets and dug foundations, creating a new community that quickly needed a nearby school. Ironically, Birch Lane was shielded from flooding because of the newly created streets and houses.

To complete the list, McKenna was completed in 1958 and originally used as a high school; Berner, in 1962, also a high school, was designed to absorb the relentless flow of students through grammar and junior high schools. Berner was built on Carman's Road, in the eastern part of Oyster Bay, on low land to the east of a creek that was originally a source of power for Carman's Mill, which stood on the site until 1911. The fact that Berner remained a high school until 1987 shows both how large the enrollment was and how it tailed off in the 1980s, allowing the district to redefine it as a junior high.

A list of school openings provided by District 23 shows the enormous growth of the system:

> *Parkside (later Ames), December 1950*
> *Unqua, February 1953*
> *East Lake, February 1953*
> *Hawthorn, September 1954*
> *Massapequa High School, September 1955*
> *Birch Lane, February 1956*
> *Carman's Road, February 1956*
> *Lockhart, February 1957*
> *McKenna Junior High School, September 1958*
> *Berner High School, January 1962*

Alfred Berner and Raymond Lockhart were responsible for construction of ten schools, including two high schools, between 1950 and 1962—including two, Ames and McKenna, that were used originally as junior highs. Lewis Ames, elected school board president in 1958, buttressed Lockhart's leadership, the latter having been named superintendent of the enlarged district in 1956. A 1960 enrollment summary and projection provided by the board of education shows why such a rapid pace of construction was necessary:

YEAR	STUDENTS
1945	*501*
1950	*1,780*
1951	*4,000*
1958	*12,446*
1964	*16,046*
1968	*15,564*[45]

The most ambitious expansion plan was floated to voters in 1956 and 1957. It consisted of an elementary school, a junior high school and a recreation/swimming pool building, along with storage facilities, located on a fifty-two-acre site along Merrick Road. Voters rejected this ambitious plan on two occasions, leading Lockhart to abandon the site. It was later purchased by the Town of Oyster Bay and redesigned as John Burns Park.

The district naturally needed teachers for the onslaught of students and recruited them aggressively. There were 30 teachers in 1945. Twenty years later, the 1964 student body was taught by 883 teachers, an astounding increase. Superintendent Herbert Pluschau remembered that many teachers were hired as temporaries or substitutes until time could be spared to observe them and assess their teaching skills. Many observations were never conducted, however, because of work pressures, and temporary teachers often were given permanent assignments because they had experience and were known by the staff. As Pluschau wrote in his essay "A Story about the Massapequa Schools 1953–1990":

> *In the 1950s and '60s the opportunity for extensive observation of a teacher's performance prior to the issuance of a probationary appointment was not the norm. Many teachers were interviewed and after transcripts and references review were offered a position. The demand for permanent staff was such that opportunity to observe the candidate teaching a class was not the norm.*[46]

A longtime beloved teacher and administrator, Wilma Diehl, was hired in 1948 at $2,400. In 1952, the starting salary was $3,000, and in 1959 it was $4,600. Wilma stayed in the system for many years, eventually becoming the first female head of the Counseling Department and later an assistant superintendent.

Donald Nobile, a current historical society trustee, was hired in 1967 at $6,250. He was one of many temporary teachers often hired after a very brief interview with an available administrator. He remained in District 23 for forty-four years.

LIBRARIES

Multibillionaire Andrew Carnegie became known for his generous support of libraries, starting in his hometown of Pittsburgh in 1890 and spreading throughout the Unites States. It is estimated that by 1930, half of all American public libraries had been built by Carnegie. In smaller communities, libraries were begun by individuals or civic-minded groups interested in providing a place for reading, book borrowing, public meetings or private reflection. Such was the case in the Massapequas, when in 1896 Civil War veteran Delancey Floyd-Jones received a grant of land from his cousin Coleman Williams to build the library that bears his name on Merrick Road across from Cedar Shore Drive.

As the school system developed in the 1950s, there were many discussions about a library system to meet the needs of children and their parents. The Floyd-Jones Library had been a popular meeting place for residents and was used by children who attended the original one-room school and the modern Massapequa School until after World War II. It remained the only library in the area, but ironically it had curtailed its hours to as few as eight per week, as Floyd-Jones family members either left the area or became unavailable to serve as librarians. The president of the school board, Alfred Berner, recommended in 1951 that a library be created to meet the needs of a growing student body and community. A committee was formed to oversee the creation of a public library system, which included a review of the status of the current library. Among the options were to retain the library as it was, namely as a private corporation, or to incorporate it into the public system through dissolution of its charter.

The original title of the committee formed in May 1952 was the Floyd-Jones Memorial Library Committee. After several meetings, members felt it necessary to separate themselves from the Floyd-Jones appellation and designated themselves as the Massapequa Public Library Committee. This suggests their sense that their system would be separate and might incorporate the Floyd-Jones Library into the public structure. Significantly, there was no mention of demolishing the building and replacing it with one or several larger libraries. In hindsight, that proved to be a unique and admirable position in view of the destruction of so many older buildings and artifacts in the Massapequas, as well as throughout Long Island.

At the same time, Floyd-Jones Library trustees met to decide how their status might be affected by the creation of a public library system. Letters were exchanged and meetings were held with the Public Library Committee, correspondence was sent to the New York secretary of state regarding the library's charter and legal opinions were expressed about the possibility of two separate libraries existing in the same location, each eligible for state funding, which amounted to $100 cash and $100 in books annually. At one point, surprisingly, the Floyd-Jones trustees indicated a willingness to give up their charter and become part of the public system, but that never happened. It became apparent that dissolution would be complicated and expensive and that the public system would then gain control over the library's endowment, which consisted of funds donated by Floyd-Jones family members over the years. Floyd-Jones Library trustees agreed to forego financial support from New York State, which allowed the public library to be created and the existing library to remain as an independent entity.

A 1952 decision of the school board created a publicly financed library system, with an initial budget of $10,000 and a temporary location in a storefront at 526 Broadway, on the corner of Broadway and Pennsylvania Avenue. The first of the two library buildings was opened in 1956 at the corner of Pennsylvania and Central Avenues. Some insight into the need for a larger building than the Floyd-Jones Library can be gained from statistics provided by Virginia Moran, librarian at the time. By 1956, the library had five thousand registered borrowers and circulated more than six hundred books and magazines per day. The new library, to replace the original building, would have stacks for twenty-five thousand books and a children's section that could seat fifty children and hold nine thousand books.[47] By contrast, the Floyd-Jones Library had a collection of five thousand books and could only seat as many as ten people comfortably.

This first building, titled the Central Avenue Library, served new residents in the northern part of the Massapequas, but it became apparent very quickly that a second location was needed to serve the rapidly growing area south of Sunrise Highway. In 1959, the Bar Harbour Shopping Center donated a parcel of land on the west side of Harbor Lane, allowing the school district to build a second library. The library trustees submitted a request for a bond issue to finance the new building. Surprisingly, the request was defeated by 156 votes, forcing the board to rethink its strategies. After extensive discussions, several community meetings and a professional marketing campaign, voters approved the new library in October 1963. Called the Bar Harbour Library, it opened in 1965, perfectly timed to serve the community that had developed around it (e.g., Harbour Green, Biltmore Shores and Nassau Shores).

As the public library system developed, the Floyd-Jones Library continued to operate separately, and patrons continued to use its services. The library's activities can be gauged by reviewing a card file from the 1960s and 1970s that contains the names of several hundred students, whose parents signed an agreement permitting them to use the library and accepting responsibility

DELANCEY FLOYD-JONES LIBRARY

ANNUAL
BOOK and BAKE
SALE

Saturday
JUNE 12
10 am
to
4 pm

Rain date
JUNE 13
noon
to
5 pm

De Lancey Floyd-Jones Free Library
Massapequa, New York
1895

MERRICK RD. OPP. CEDAR SHORE DR.
MASSAPEQUA, N.Y.

BOOKS ~ BAKED GOODS ~ ART EXHIBIT
VISITING CLOWNS ~ PLANTS
and more ~

WELCOME ALL!

Delancey Floyd-Jones Library bake sale, 1975. *Courtesy of Delancey Floyd-Jones Free Library.*

for the timely and safe return of books. The modern, larger and up-to-date public system steadily attracted more users, as was expected. A Friends of the Floyd-Jones Library group was formed in 1970, growing to almost two hundred members, to raise money through fund drives, bake sales, tours and other activities, in order to meet continuing expenses and continue to attract patrons. These efforts had a positive short-term effect, but by the mid-1980s, many Friends had either moved away or withdrawn their support. Fewer students and residents frequented the archaic and inadequate building.

Louisa (Floyd-Jones) Thorn Bonner, the last Floyd-Jones family member attached to the library, resigned as board chair in 1985, raising the possibility that the building would continue to slide into disuse and disrepair. Fortunately, Eugene Bryson, a longtime Massapequa resident and a Grace Church vestryman, accepted the position of board chairman. He supervised its physical renovation, including redesigning the back room, used originally as a storage area, to hold library shelves and hired a librarian to refresh the collection. He also had the building repurposed as a historic building, earning it Town of Oyster Bay historic status in 2000. His efforts breathed new life into a building that is one of the oldest in the area and remains an important part of Massapequa's past.

Visitors to the library may not check out books but are welcome to visit and review the collections. Among the favorites are the Hardy Boys, Nancy Drew and Tom Swift series. Visitors may also review the file of parental permissions. Several visitors who have returned as adults have found their parental agreement forms and have taken copies. The library is open on Wednesdays and Saturdays from 10:00 a.m. to 1:00 p.m. and continues as a place for research, reminiscence and relaxation.

RELIGIOUS WORSHIP

Protestant

For many years, there was only one church in the Massapequas, namely Old Grace Episcopal Church on Merrick Road, which had celebrated its 100th birthday in 1944. It also felt the pressure of growth, as it became far too small for the growing population. It was built as the Floyd-Jones summer church and expanded in 1905 but could hold only about 100 worshipers. Active membership of 141 worshipers was documented in 1939, along with 136 Sunday school students. By the mid-1950s, it had become too small for the growing congregation (520 communicants in 1950; 1,709 in 1960), so its vestry members followed the typical pattern of raising funds, buying property and designing a larger church to meet parishioners' needs.

A lot directly across Merrick Road (donated to the church by John D. Jones in 1880 and farmed by, among others, the Kicherer family) was purchased, and the "new" Grace Church was constructed, opening in 1962, for a congregation that had grown to more than three thousand by then. Appropriately, a Floyd-Jones mansion dating back to the 1880s existed on the property and was moved so the church would be seen from Merrick Road. It had been used as the rectory as far back as the 1890s and continued to be used for that purpose. A school was built in 1963.

Old Grace Church leaders, urged by Father Wiley, had created a chapel in 1895 in northwest Massapequa for the farming population there. It was originally designated as Grace Church Chapel but was renamed St. Christopher's Episcopal Chapel in 1952 and was given its own priest. Later additions included a meeting hall and a Sunday school building. It served the large farming community until the 1960s, by which time almost all the farms were sold for housing sites. The congregation dwindled until, in 1980, the Episcopal Church sold the building to the Greek Orthodox Church, which renamed it St. Gregory of Nyssa Church.

Another postwar church has its own unusual history. Originally built in 1873, the Bellport Methodist Church stood on Brown's Lane and Maple Street in Bellport, Long Island. In 1945, the expanding Methodist congregation moved into a nearby Presbyterian church, and the Brooklyn-Long Island Methodist Council informed Massapequa Methodists that the building was available and was movable. Local worshipers, who had held their services in the Massapequa Fire Department and the American Legion Hall, raised the funds needed for the tricky journey from Bellport to Massapequa. The twenty-six-by-forty-four-foot church was moved off its foundation, placed on greased wooden skids and rolled one mile down to Great South Bay. It was then put on a barge and floated to Jones Creek to be unloaded. Timing is everything, however, and the barge got stuck in the mud by the shore (today's Burns Park) for six hours, until the tide rose enough for workers to transfer the building onto a truck for the half-mile trip to its current location. The eighteen-foot steeple was detached and shipped separately, to minimize interference with wires and trees.

The site chosen by the Methodist congregation had its own important history. It was, for many years, the site of the only school building, the one-room (and, after 1910, two-room) schoolhouse used by students from 1870 until 1925. For the subsequent twenty years, the building was used as a utility and storage site by the school district. Massapequa Methodists bought the site for $2,500, tore down the school and contracted with the Kicherer firm

Community Methodist
Church on South Oyster Bay.
*Courtesy of the Historical Society
of the Massapequas.*

to dig out a basement and pour a new foundation. Once that was completed, the building was moved to the site and set with the entrance facing Park Boulevard. It was named Community United Methodist Church.

Anybody who visits the site today, however, would be confused because the church runs north–south, paralleling Park Boulevard, with the altar on the south side. The reason is another example of the enormous growth of the Massapequas in the 1950s. By the end of the decade, the congregation had grown to 1,500 members, far too large for the small church. A building committee was established and oversaw construction of a new sanctuary, running north–south, along with Sunday school and meeting rooms. The original church, known among old-time members as the "Bellport Church," became a meeting hall and retains that function today.

The church developed an admirable reputation for challenging existing prejudices by inviting Black residents from East Massapequa to worship and by appointing Reverend McQuay Kiah as its first Black assistant pastor. Some residents objected to this challenge to the status quo, burning a cross on one member's lawn, throwing rocks through windows of other members and writing racist slurs on their cars. Despite this shameful behavior (or perhaps because of it), the church flourished, filling its new sanctuary and its meeting hall, which was the original "Bellport Church," for many years.[48]

As the Community United Methodist Church grew, another Protestant church was forming north of Sunrise Highway. In early 1950, Daniel Lehman, a Lutheran who had recently moved into the area, approached the United Lutheran Synod of New York about beginning a church. In June of that year, the synod created St. David's Lutheran Church. A pastor was assigned and services were held in Massapequa Park's Village Hall. About seventy members attended Sunday services, and there were about twenty students in the Sunday school. As the Village Hall became too crowded (members had to stand outside and listen to the service), services were moved to Parkside (later Ames) School and were occasionally held in a local doctor's office.

In early 1952, the congregation purchased lots on the corner of Lakeshore Drive and Clark Boulevard for $11,800. Subsequent fundraising activities provided enough money for a church building to be completed during that year. Membership continued to grow, reaching 587 by July 1955, with a Sunday school enrollment of 650. The original building quickly became too small, and a larger one was completed in 1962. About $300,000 was raised to complete the new church, which had room for four hundred members.[49]

These two churches set the pattern followed by many others in the Massapequas. The First Baptist Church opened in 1951 at 89 Parkhill Avenue at the corner of Hicksville Road. The building was expanded in 1960 with the assistance of the pastor, Harry Hobart, who did much of the carpentry, while other volunteers used their electrical and plumbing skills to save costs. The church had a small congregation at that time—forty parishioners—so they needed to tap into their talents to build a permanent structure. Pastor Hobart estimated the total cost to be $40,000, a small amount even at that time and astonishingly small from our current vantage point.

The Presbyterian denomination brought an unusual history to the establishment of the Presbyterian Community Church on Pittsburgh Avenue. There was a small Presbyterian church located on Parkhill Avenue for a few years, but it closed in the late 1930s and the building eventually came to house the Massapequa Republican Club. After the war, many new residents approached the Brooklyn-Nassau Presbytery about creating a new church. A meeting at the American Legion Hall in July 1950 identified twenty-eight members. They were recognized by the presbytery and began to hold services, first in a small church on Broadway and later at the adjacent Lockhart School. In September 1951, a Sunday school was organized, and one hundred students registered.

As the congregation grew, its leaders sought out land for a church complex. They bought several parcels on Pittsburgh Avenue and built a Fellowship Hall and a Sunday school. In 1956, a capital plan was devised and a building fund was established, leading to $165,000 in pledges for a church building. Construction began in early 1961, and the sanctuary was completed in September. The congregation continued to grow, as did the Sunday school, the latter reaching an enrollment of one thousand students by the late 1960s. A nursery school was established in 1958 and continues to this day.

A small unpretentious church was built in the middle of Massapequa Park to provide worship space for members of the Nazarene denomination, who had moved to the Massapequas and to adjacent communities. A lot on the corner of Roosevelt Avenue and Wilson Street was purchased, and the leadership of the New York Church of the Nazarene set about attracting a congregation and raising funds. The first service was held on October 2, 1952, in Massapequa Park Village Hall with 136 in attendance. Subsequent services were held there and at East Lake School, where a Sunday school was also established. By 1956, enough money was available to build a wood-framed church, and construction began under the direction of Reverend Ralph Montemuro. The first service at the Church of the Nazarene was held on June 6 in a building that included a sanctuary for 100 members, a Sunday school room, a small apartment, a kitchen, restrooms and a small nursery room.

The congregation continued to grow, and a plot of land adjacent to the original church was purchased in 1972. Eleven years later, the new, larger church was built and included a fellowship room in the basement. It also contained air conditioning, making it difficult for members to claim that it was uncomfortable to attend services in the summer months! Reverends Ann and Anderson Rearick led the church through the '80s.

The Massapequa Reformed Church on Ocean Avenue and Merrick Road was built a few years later, through the efforts of worshipers from other Reformed churches who had moved to the Massapequas. Starting in 1962, they began holding services in Unqua School and then in the American Legion Hall. In the latter instance, members replaced the picture of President John Kennedy with that of Jesus during services.

In 1963, the Fraser property just north of Merrick Road was purchased and used as a church, school, meeting hall and social center. The building was designated as a church in 1964, to serve 99 members. By 1966, that number had grown to 200, and they purchased the lot south of the Fraser house, completing a new church building by 1968 to seat 198. Funds came from members, other Reformed churches and donors who supported an additional church in the area. The Fraser house was subsequently refitted as a preschool. The Massapequa Reformed Church was the last Protestant place of worship to be built in this area in the heady days after World War II.[50]

Roman Catholic

Many new Massapequans were Roman Catholic, and they soon realized there was no Catholic church in the area. The few Catholics who lived in the area before 1945 would have attended either St. William the Abbot Church in Seaford (1928) or St. Martin's Church in Amityville (1897). The Brooklyn Diocese originally served Long Island, but a separate diocese was created in 1957 and installed at Rockville Center. Its leader, Bishop Walter Kellenberg, recognized the explosive growth of the Massapequas as well as other Long Island communities and moved quickly to provide structures for St. Rose of Lima Church, which was created in 1952.

By 1952, the parish encompassed 1,900 families, and Masses were held in the former Wagon Wheel Restaurant on Merrick Road, originally the Floyd-Jones mansion dating back to the late 1800s and called Holland House. It was redesigned to hold 600 worshipers, and around 1,700 members attended its four Masses on Sundays. Diocesan leaders gave priority to education and built a school to the east of the temporary church, opening it in 1960 for grades one through six (expanded to eight grades in 1963). Shortly thereafter, ground was broken for a church to serve the more than 2,500 families. It was completed in 1965 and blessed by Bishop Kellenberg. The site of the Wagon Wheel building is today the parking lot located between the church and school.[51]

The geography of the Massapequas made St. Rose of Lima somewhat inconvenient for the many Catholics who settled north of Sunrise Highway and throughout Massapequa Park. Our Lady of Lourdes Church was begun in 1955. The property was a six-acre farm owned by Michael Forte, who sold it, a farmhouse and three buildings to what was then still the Brooklyn Diocese. One building was used as a rectory, one as a convent, one as a chapel and the farmhouse as a school until the new building was completed.

The emphasis in this area was also on education, and a cornerstone for what became Our Lady of Lourdes School was laid in 1961 off Carman's Road, just south of the Southern State Parkway. The building with twenty-four classrooms, an auditorium and a cafeteria, as well as a convent and chapel, opened in September 1962. Church services were held at Hawthorn, Carman's Road and East Lake Schools for many years, minimizing the need for a church building. Surprisingly, Our Lady of Lourdes Church was not completed until 1985, by which time the school was well established and was drawing students from the Massapequas, Amityville and Farmingdale.

The Old Barn

... becomes THE FIRST CHAPEL

Our Lady of Lourdes Chapel, 1955. *Courtesy of the Historical Society of the Massapequas.*

Jewish

Three temples served as worship centers for the Jewish community in the Massapequas. The first was Temple Judea, begun by members who met originally in the back of Bob Mann's Shoe Store on Broadway in 1951. They later used the Community Methodist Church, Grace Episcopal Church and the Hicksville Road Firehouse for worship services. Like many other religious organizations, their primary focus was on education, as seen by the chronology of using Grace Church for its first school of 103 students and later using public school facilities.

Known then as the Massapequa Jewish Center, the members opened an eight-room schoolhouse on Jerusalem Avenue in 1955 and completed a Temple building in 1962. The congregation changed its name to Temple Judea in 1970 and continued as an independent organization until 2007, when it affiliated with a Jewish temple in Wantagh to become Temple B'nai Torah. This procedure followed a common pattern among Jewish worship sites: two or more merged into one because of the dwindling numbers of congregants toward the end of the century. This process was ably documented by Rhoda Miller in *The Jewish Community of Long Island.*

Temple Beth-El members wandered throughout the Massapequas in the 1950s—worshiping in a congregant's home, in Old Grace Church and in a storefront on Jerusalem Avenue—until they were able to purchase a site on Jerusalem Avenue east of Hicksville Road. The cornerstone of its building is dated 1961, when the Temple finally completed construction of its worship space, as well as a meeting hall and offices.

Temple Sinai, located in East Massapequa, is the other long-established Jewish worship site in the area. Located originally in Amityville, its members built a new house of worship in 1958 toward the southern end of Clocks Boulevard as a member of the Union of Reformed Judaism. Statistics bear out the expansion of the Jewish population in the Massapequas, as well as throughout Nassau County, and the resulting need for worship sites. From only 17,300 in 1940, the Jewish population in the county exploded to 155,000 in 1950, 345,000 in 1960, 372,000 in 1970 and 395,000 in 1980. The downward trend then began, leading to the closure and/or merger of worship sites: 311,000 total population in 1990 and 207,000 in 1998, the last date for which figures are available.[52]

There was another church in the area prior to World War II, and that was the Christian Science Church, built on Merrick Road across from Massapequa Lake in 1934. The church had taken over a real estate building established by the Fox Frankel Corporation, which was constructing and marketing Spanish-style houses in Biltmore Shores south of Merrick Road. The building had a similar Spanish style, but the leaders replaced it with a red brick building to house an office, meeting hall and reading room. It remained active until 2007, when it was replaced by St. Peter's and St. Paul's Malankara Jacobite Orthodox Church.

SHOPPING

There were a few stores along Merrick Road and Broadway built before World War I, and the small population did not require larger centers. The first enterprise that could be considered a shopping center was a series of six two-story buildings joined together west of Hicksville Road and built by the Fraser Company in 1938. These proved adequate until the postwar population explosion. Then, in 1958, the Bar Harbour Shopping Center was completed, a mall with more than forty stores, providing clothing, shoes, housewares and hardware. There were several restaurants and ample parking for many cars. Its popularity grew in the 1960s, leading developers to decide to build a multi-story mall, as had been done in Valley Stream, Garden City (Roosevelt Field) and Huntington (Walt Whitman Mall). They selected a swampy, unkempt area just north of Sunrise Highway in East Massapequa. The area, called familiarly "The Pit," was used by children for hunting frogs, fishing in the small streams and hiding in the overgrowth. It also became a location where large waste, including old cars, was dumped. The area was filled in, and the mall opened in 1973, named the Sunrise Mall. It was anchored by several large stores, the first being Macy's. Later stores included Abraham and Straus, J.C. Penney and Sears. It occupied two floors and opened a multiplex movie theater in 1976. The theaters closed in 2000, and the mall has gone through many changes, including different ownership and replacement of the "anchor" stores.

The Bar Harbour Shopping Center suffered after the Sunrise Mall opened and was redesigned in the late 1970s. The back portion was turned into the Bar Harbour Condominiums, the theater that occupied the second floor was closed and the number of shops was reduced to allow for additional parking. Anchor stores such as Saks 34th Street and Gimbels were closed because they couldn't compete against the anchor stores in Sunrise Mall. The largest store became the supermarket site that is today occupied by King Kullen.

MOVIES

Pequa Cinema, circa 1980. *Courtesy of the Historical Society of the Massapequas.*

On September 19, 1941, *Newsday* highlighted movies showing in several Long Island theaters—in Glen Cove, Hempstead, Freeport (two theaters), Lynbrook (two theaters) and Rockville Center. There was none listed for Massapequa because theaters were not opened here until the 1950s. The first to open was the Massapequa Drive-In, begun in 1951, on land behind Frank Buck's Zoo. It remained open for several months each year and closed in 1966. Indoor theaters were built in the Bar Harbour Shopping Center (1960), in the Carman's Road Shopping Center and in a small shopping center on the corner of Hicksville Road and Jerusalem Avenue. A modern and spacious theater, called the Pequa, opened in 1964 on Sunrise Highway, east of Broadway. It featured an all-glass lobby and exposed ceiling joists. It showed first-run films and was popular until 1989, when it fell victim, as did most other single-screen theaters, to multiplexes.

Perhaps the most intriguing theater was the one run by Jerry Lewis, the enormously successful comedian from the 1950s, who created a chain of small theaters in 1972, with two hundred seats, that were supposed to be simple to run and maintain by franchisees. Lewis's backers never provided training or financial support for theater owners, and he lost interest in the project. His theater closed in 1980 and is today the site of the Staples Store, at the end of what was the Frank Buck Zoo.

PARKS

The Town of Oyster Bay responded to the influx of homeowners by opening Tobay Beach in 1960. Jones Beach to the west was very crowded, and the town leaders were interested in providing an area restricted to town residents. The one-mile stretch to the east of Jones Beach belonged to the town as the result of an 1805 court decision that reserved that part of the Jones domain to the town. Robert Moses was unable to break through the decision in the 1920s and so left the beach untouched. The town built a main building in the center and two smaller service buildings to the west and the east, the latter at the border with Suffolk County. It also developed a wading beach along South Oyster Bay for the convenience of small children.

The Massapequa Park trustees built Brady Park north of the LIRR tracks and west of Lakeshore Drive, so children could play ball and use the playground and their parents could picnic or just relax beside the reservoir. It also created Mansfield Park, west of Lakeshore Drive and near Linden Street. It was supposed to be developed with a swimming pool run by the Village, to compete with the pools at Marjorie Post Park, but it became evident very soon that the water table was too high, as the property stood east of the Massapequa Preserve with its streams and lakes. The park is used by baseball and soccer teams today.

John Burns was supervisor for the Town of Oyster Bay from 1958 to 1962 and became alarmed at the increase of private housing without suitable recreation areas for residents. He latched onto a fifty-two-acre parcel that was scheduled to hold 640 new homes and convinced Governor Nelson Rockefeller, Nassau County executive A. Holly Patterson and Robert Moses to condemn the land and buy it for $1 million. The town eventually created a multi-use site (ballfields, playgrounds, handball courts and more) and named it John Burns Park.

THE MASSAPEQUA PRESERVE

The Preserve is a 488-acre green space running from Merrick Road north to Linden Street, dividing Massapequa Park from the rest of Massapequa. It was originally purchased by Brooklyn, a separate city, in the 1880s and taken over by New York City when it incorporated Brooklyn in 1898. The city built a system to supply water to Brooklyn, using a series of reservoirs connected by water mains under what became Sunrise Highway. The lake in Brady Park, for example, is still officially named the Massapequa Reservoir. In 1930, Massapequa took control of its own water and pumped it through a system of local wells and pipes. The city was able to tap into the Long Island supply in 1965–66, during an extended drought, but otherwise had little interest in its original system. By 1980, when New York City was experiencing serious financial stress, Mayor Edward Koch contacted Nassau

County about selling off the system, and County Executive Francis Purcell bought it for $6.7 million.

Massapequa Park was able to acquire rights to the northern 350 acres of what was then called Massapequa State Park in 1965 and added that parcel to the acreage just described, creating what is today the Massapequa Preserve. The title is important because it underscores that the property is to be *preserved* as an open space. Two developments that confirm that design are the 7.4-mile bicycle path that runs from Merrick Road all the way into Bethpage State Park and the Nassau-Suffolk Greenbelt Trail, a 22-mile hiking path from Merrick Road to Cold Spring Harbor. Both paths were created in 1981 to provide differing recreation activities for residents and visitors. The Preserve has two lakes north of the reservoir and a fishing bridge built by the Kiwanis Club and contains Brady Park and Mansfield Park. It is maintained by the Friends of Massapequa Preserve, headed by Lisa and Richard Schary. The Preserve was named the Peter J. Schmitt Massapequa Preserve in 2013 in honor of the late Nassau County legislator.

LONG ISLAND RAIL ROAD STATIONS

The Babylon branch of the Long Island Rail Road underwent significant changes as the Massapequas and the surrounding south shore experienced significant population growth. The line had run at ground level, but it became apparent very quickly that that design was becoming increasingly dangerous with the growth of pedestrian and automobile traffic. The Massapequa station was elevated in 1953, Merrick in 1970 and all other stations by 1975—with the exception of the Massapequa Park station. Originally a whistle stop by Grand Avenue, the Massapequa Park station was created east of Park Boulevard in 1933. It consisted of two small wooden sheds with a ticket agent's office on the westbound side. The buildings were extended after the war and the tracks raised in the early '60s to accommodate larger and higher trains, but Park Boulevard remained at ground level, resulting in several accidents and deaths. By the early 1970s, the Village mayor and trustees had become convinced of the need to raise the station. Several residents had objected to the elevation from the beginning and demonstrated publicly against the plan to destroy the rural character of the Village, as they characterized it.

The Metropolitan Transportation Authority had taken over the LIRR from the Pennsylvania system, which went bankrupt in 1966. Elevated service was recognized as important, but it was difficult to obtain funds, especially because of the issues raised by the 1973 energy crisis and the sharp decline in New York City revenues. With the aid of the federal government and New York State, the MTA pegged the station elevation cost at $15–20 million and let out bids in 1976. Costs rose because of unexpected expenses. The electrical lines laid along Front Street from Park Boulevard to Unqua Road in the 1930s needed to be replaced. Sunrise Highway needed to be rerouted, creating significant complaints from the community. Robert Thompson was mayor and insisted on high-quality workmanship. In one instance, Massapequa Park engineers rejected concrete poured for the sides of the elevated station because it was substandard. Rebars were added to subsequent pourings. In another, Thompson insisted that Massapequa Park control all signage put up on either side of the elevated station.

All these issues stretched out the project and raised costs, so that New York State ending up earmarking $30 million in its 1980 budget to complete the project. The first passengers used the elevated station on Saturday, December 13, 1980. Work was completed in October 1981, and the total cost was identified as $35 million. Massapequa Park thus became the last station elevated on the Babylon branch.[53]

Chapter 8

PRESERVING, RECORDING AND PROMOTING THE PAST

The Historical Society of the Massapequas is tasked with keeping records and artifacts of the area's history, as well as making them accessible to the public. The name is reflective of the different parts of the Massapequas and was adopted after spirited debate in the society's early years. The society represents Massapequa, geographically in the center, as well as East Massapequa, which had its own zip code until 1978; North Massapequa, which has its own fire department; and the incorporated Village of Massapequa Park. Residents are quick to correct anybody who does not identify their residence correctly.

The origins of the historical society are crystal clear. There was talk in the 1930s of creating a society in connection with efforts to save Tryon Hall (Fort Neck House), and some observers have stated that it grew in response to attempts to tear down Little Unqua in the late 1950s, but there is no evidence of an organized effort, of meetings, of notices in the press and other media or of activities designed to attract local politicians to save the estate. A firm date is 1969, when Anne Markiewicz enlisted her friend Lorraine Newman to speak out publicly about two acts of vandalism to Old Grace Church that summer. Youngsters had twice broken into the building, damaged the altar rail and pulpit and threw papers around the center aisle. The incidents attracted public attention, and Ms. Markiewicz and Ms. Newman convinced State Assemblyman Philip Healey to grant a provisional charter, establishing an organization titled the Massapequa Historical Society.

Grace Church damage, 1969. *Courtesy of the Historical Society of the Massapequas.*

Nothing further is known about the society for a decade. The 1976 bicentennial celebrations in the area did not include mention of it. The Village of Massapequa Park formed a historical committee to organize parades and festivities in early July, but the historical society was not listed in any accounts of sponsors and/or participants. Kathy Hayes was listed as village historian but appears to have acted solely with other Massapequa Park residents to promote the festivities.

The year 1978 was the date when the society was resurrected, over the status of Old Grace Church. The older church was used rarely for services and had fallen into disrepair. The pastor, Father John Jobson, and the church vestry debated what to do, because they could not justify spending money to maintain a building for which they had no use. It was 135 years old and one of the oldest buildings in the area, and there was a real possibility that it would be torn down. The stained-glass windows, in fact, were removed for placement in the Grace Church sanctuary across the street.

Anne Markiewicz deserves credit for leading resistance to this position and eventually retaining the building for the community. Ms. Markiewicz sounded the alarm throughout the Massapequas and attracted many residents who were also worried about the church, including current Grace Church members, who had been baptized there, attended services, were married there and even had their children worship there. They met with the vestry several times, held rallies, organized town meetings, attracted the support of local politicians and eventually became large enough to raise the possibility of taking over the building. The date of May 15, 1981, was

Anne Markiewicz with Assemblyman Philip Healey. *Courtesy of the Historical Society of the Massapequas.*

set for demolition of the building, but the vestry was sympathetic to the historical society's proposal and leased and later sold the building, as well as six feet of ground around it, to the historical society for ten dollars, under a twenty-five-year lease. Grace Church was thus relieved of a burden as well as negative publicity, and the historical society took on an important project.[54]

Historical society members began the arduous process of reviving Old Grace Church, holding festivals (including two Preservathons) in front of the building and making repairs as needed. They replaced the shingles and added a new roof, the latter thanks to the generosity of the United Carpenters' Union. The most dramatic renovation was the replacement of the church's windows with those from an Episcopal church in Delaware, New Jersey, that was scheduled for demolition. The windows were slightly wider and needed to be resized, but the process was completed by 1986 and the new windows were installed. Donors paid $2,000 for each window, and the society raised additional funds as necessary. All donors were recognized with a plaque fixed at the bottom of their respective window. The window behind the altar was returned by Grace Church and reinstalled.

Another early project was the relocation of the Floyd-Jones coachman's cottage (later renamed the servants' cottage) from its location west of the Bar Harbour Library. The cottage had been rented for many years after Elbert Floyd-Jones's wife died in 1918, first by the Gottert family (Charles was Queens County sheriff) and later by Helen Bagnall, a prominent member of Grace Church, who installed electricity and indoor plumbing in the late 1940s. It was occupied briefly by the Baldwin family of acting fame, while their house was repaired after a fire. It was vacant by the early 1980s and had suffered from vandalism, as well as occupation by a family of raccoons. The Cummings family bought the property in 1983 and were approached by the historical society, whose officers proposed to move the building close to the old church. The family wanted the building removed and gave the society time to raise funds. The usual methods were employed: fundraisers, along with appeals to local officials and to the general community.

"Save Old Grace Church" flyer. *Courtesy of the Historical Society of the Massapequas.*

Old Grace Church. *Courtesy of the Historical Society of the Massapequas.*

By 1986, the historical society had raised enough money to pay Davis Engineering to move the decaying structure across Merrick Road onto a piece of property next to the Grace Church Cemetery donated by Floyd-Jones library trustees. The foundation was laid by the Kicherer Company, and the building was moved in July. The main concern was that the fragile building might fall apart in the middle of Merrick Road, but that did not occur. The movers were careful to remove the chimney and the roof to fit the cottage under electric wires and were able to secure the building onto its new foundation without incident.

As with Old Grace Church, the old cottage needed much work. It was essentially gutted, and new floors and walls were built. The basement was cemented, a new electrical system was installed and a center stairwell was erected, covering over what had been a root cellar. This process took almost twenty years until the structure could be opened to the public. Complicating the process were two acts of vandalism that occurred in February 1988, both of which severely damaged the interior. The vandals were never caught, but the incident lengthened the restoration process. Fourth graders from nearby Fairfield School held a Walkathon and raised $6,500 to aid the restoration, and other residents contributed.[55]

To enhance the cottage's restoration, society members and local residents donated furnishings to give it the appearance of an early twentieth-century residence. There are features such as a water pump, washboards, metal bathtubs, coffee grinders, a small four-burner stove and an icebox in the kitchen. A piano, a typewriter, a child's high chair, a sewing machine and old table settings are located in what was the living room. On the other side of the stairs, another room has photos of the Massapequas at different times and documents describing the Massapequa Hotel and Native American tools discovered in the area over the years. Prominently displayed over the mantel is a composite of the mansions that existed in the Massapequas for many years.

The society stores its important files and business records in one of the upper rooms and is involved in a process to digitize the paper records for posterity. The files represent important sources for the history of the area and have been used by several trustees in their research work.

Larger souvenirs, including farm implements, are kept in the cottage's basement. The original building had only a root cellar, located under the stairs, but society trustees foresaw the need to have a much larger storage space for larger implements, as well as holiday decorations and artifacts that are unsuited for display in Old Grace Church. The cottage has a heating and ventilation system but no water. Most of the repairs were done by historical society trustees and volunteers, who donated much time and talent to the effort.

The historical society's history was marked with one especially bitter and trying incident, namely the use of Grace Church Cemetery for festivals. The society held strawberry festivals in June and apple festivals in October, allowing vendors to sell their wares. These festivals, as well as occasional flower sales on Mother's Day and a Corn Festival in August 1985, brought in money the society used for repairs. In the late 1980s, Grace Church vestry members objected to these events, characterizing them as carnival-type activities that did not belong on church property. Discussions went on for more than a year, with the society even holding a festival against an express prohibition by the vestry. Both sides employed attorneys to fight their cases and were moving toward a trial when cooler heads prevailed.

John Venditto, a Massapequa native and later Town of Oyster Bay supervisor, was the town attorney in 1991 and brought the two sides to his office. After much discussion, the sides agreed to a compromise that allowed the historical society to continue its festivals, with close supervision of the vendors. Overlooked in this dispute was the fact that the church had sold burial plots on the east side of the church from the mid-1980s, in violation of the original lease. After the settlement, it continued to sell plots on either side of Grace Church, extending them in front of the building, thereby reducing the number of vendors the historical society could attract. The historical society has sought other sources of revenue and continues as an active and important part of the Massapequa community.

The society recently became conservator of the Jones family cemetery (also called West Neck Cemetery) on Merrick Road east of Massapequa Avenue. The cemetery was neglected for many years, mainly because

Historical Society of the Massapequas

OLD GRACE CHURCH

FLOYD-JONES
SERVANTS' COTTAGE

DELANCEY FLOYD-
JONES FREE LIBRARY

Massapequa's Historic Complex. *Author's collection.*

nobody knew who owned it. Town of Oyster Bay records could not be found documenting ownership. Supervisor Venditto encouraged the historical society to become its conservator and agreed that the town would provide regular maintenance. The society cleared the ground of trees and shrubs and erected a wrought-iron fence and a metal sign identifying it in 2016. The cemetery dates from the 1760s and contains the remains of more than forty Jones family members, including Colonel Benjamin Birdsall and Samuel Jones, both commemorated by special markers.

Jones (West Neck) Cemetery. *Author's collection.*

Another significant historical society endeavor was the creation of several markers throughout the area to serve as reminders of its history. The idea was first broached by Arlene Goodenough, society president, in 1985. She felt it would be important and appropriate to erect a marker in recognition of Thomas Jones and convinced society trustees to place it at Jones Beach. Jones Beach for many centuries looked nothing like it does today. The area was really a thin strand of beach that was breached several times, creating islands that rejoined and separated as subsequent storms moved the sand along the shore. It took the herculean efforts of another driven, daring and successful leader to create the beach that the historical society honored.

Robert Moses had become secretary of the New York State Association (an obscure position that cloaked his close political affiliation with Governor Al Smith and Mayor Jimmy Walker) in the early 1920s and was obsessed with improving the lives of New Yorkers, both in the city and throughout the state, by creating a transportation network and a series of parks and recreation areas. He moved to Babylon and took many trips around Long Island, looking for an appropriate target for his ideas. He finally settled on the former Jones holdings bordering the Atlantic Ocean, by then owned by the State of New York.

Robert Caro, in his monumental book *The Power Broker*, describes how Moses connived with local politicians and business leaders and cajoled nearby residents to allow him to create roads that would lead to a beach he felt would dwarf any that existed anywhere. He filled in the inlets that often opened along the shoreline, creating a six-mile stretch of pure white sand. He built bathhouses grander than any ever seen before, a boardwalk along the entire length of the beach, playgrounds, huge parking lots, restaurants and snack bars and a beach large enough to accommodate several hundred thousand visitors. He also created the Wantagh State Parkway and the Meadowbrook State Parkway, to both expedite travel throughout Nassau County and especially attract car owners from New York City, as well as Nassau County. By 1928, his vision had become reality, and the Jones Beach we all know today opened to huge crowds, grateful to escape from the stifling heat of New York City in the summer.

Had Thomas Jones seen the result of Moses's efforts, he would have understood how ambition can drive people to go far beyond accepted limits. These two men were remarkably alike in their daring and determination to make something out of what appeared to be nothing. The historical society recognized Jones's accomplishments (and implicitly Moses's) by placing its first marker at the entrance to the beach in 1985. The marker is located in the ground near the bus stop south of the Jones Tower. It reads:

Major Thomas Jones
Born in Ireland c. 1665
Died 1713. Buried in Massapequa
Settled in Fort Neck Now Massapequa
In 1696 with wife Freelove Townsend.
Owned 6000 acres on Long Island
Established a whaling station
On this beach.

It then reprinted the epitaph from his tombstone:

From distant lands to
This wild waste he came
This seat he chose and
There he fixed his name
Long may his sons this
Peaceful spot enjoy
And no ill fate his
Offspring here annoy

The historical society has subsequently erected seventeen additional markers, with blue backgrounds and yellow text, mounted on seven-foot metal poles. Many are located along Merrick Road because that was the only major road in the area for many years and the site of Massapequa's mansions. In chronological order by placement, the markers are:

- *West Neck (Jones) Cemetery, 1988*
- *Tryon Hall, 1992*
- *Old Brick House, 1993*
- *1796 Hotel Site, 1993*
- *Farm District, 1994*
- *Carman's Mill, 1995*[56]
- *Flying Field, 1995*
- *Thorn Estate, 1998*
- *Woodcastle Hotel, 2000*
- *Massapequa Hotel, 2008*
- *Killian's Hotel, 2009*
- *First Fire House, 2010*
- *Historic Complex, 2011*
- *Red House, 2012*
- *Frank Buck Zoo, 2014*
- *Massapequa School, 2015*
- *Massapequa Manor, 2016*

Chapter 9

UNUSUAL AND UNEXPECTED

Why is there a statue of a Native American on Sunrise Highway? The figure—flanked by a horse, a buffalo and a totem pole—was commissioned by real estate developer R.J. Lewis, who was attracted to Native Americans and their history. He had the figures designed and erected in fiberglass to honor those who lived here before white settlement. The statues were erected in 1968. Legend has it that anybody who touches the totem pole while making a wish will have that wish come true. Lewis renamed himself Big Chief Lewis, even though he was not Native American, and the sign is still on top of the building he erected for his businesses in the 1950s.

Anybody who attended Massapequa High School is familiar with the term "Polio Pond." The term refers to a small pond to the east of the school that drained under Merrick Road to South Oyster Bay. It was felt that the water was dangerous and could cause polio because it was stagnant and carried bacteria. The high school was completed in 1955, the same year a vaccine developed by Dr. Jonas Salk was approved for general use. As a result of a massive campaign led by the March of Dimes, the number of polio cases in the United States dropped from 35,000 in 1953 to 161 in 1961. The term has remained, however, and students still view the pond with some concern.

A fierce rivalry developed between Berner High School and Massapequa High School, culminating in a Thanksgiving Day football game pitting the

Berner Bisons against the Massapequa Chiefs and attended by thousands of spectators. One personal vignette involves a historical society trustee, whose boyfriend (later husband) wanted to come to her house to visit or to take her out. The woman had two older brothers, and they attended Massapequa. Her boyfriend attended Berner. They decided that he could come inside, but he was required to leave his Berner jacket outside on the porch. After the couple married, they argued about whether to live near Massapequa or Berner until they realized that the only house they could afford was near Massapequa High.

There is a barn along Hicksville Road just south of the Southern State Parkway. It seems out of place next to all the private houses, but it is a reminder that the area was the Farm District for many years. The barn holds old farm implements and car parts. It looks fragile and rickety but deserves mention because it can alert residents and passersby, as well as readers, to the huge changes that have occurred in the Massapequas over the past century.

Most of the waterways in the Massapequas are shallow, but there is one location that is unusually deep. It is located behind St. Peter's and St. Paul's Malankara Jacobite Orthodox Church on Merrick Road and was dredged out to 125 feet in the late 1920s. The church building was back then Fox and Frankel's real estate office. The company dug out the river and designed a beach around it, complete with several diving boards, including one high board. Olympic swimmer Johnny Weissmuller was among the celebrities employed to attract patrons. Despite extensive publicity, the company was unable to attract enough customers to pay its expenses, and it folded in the 1930s. The real estate office was replaced by the Christian Science Church, and the beach was covered over by docks and mooring sites, as boat owners settled along Massapequa's waterways after World War II.

Residents who had moved to the Massapequas after World War I could take up the unusual sport of lawn bowling, using a court built by Robert Moses in the 1920s northeast of the Massapequa train station. The women wore white linen dresses and the men white pants and white wingtip shoes. They rolled a ball about the size of a grapefruit at pins located at the end of the green. The sport became popular in the 1930s but lost its appeal during the war, as so many residents were in the armed forces. The court was replaced in 1950 by a Little League ballfield, baseball having a much stronger attraction to newly arrived youngsters than lawn bowling. The first baseball Little League was formed in 1939, and the sport's popularity exploded after World War II.

Several houses were moved into and around the Massapequas in the past fifty years. One of the more interesting moves involved relocating the Bowery Savings Bank in January 1973 from its location on Sunrise Highway to Brady Park, where it was to become a community center. The Village of Massapequa Park oversaw the move, which went smoothly until the yoke connecting the building to the trailer broke in the middle of Sunrise Highway. Village representatives frantically looked for welders and additional moving help, and the building was eventually moved to Brady Park. Complicating the situation was the fact that the Long Island Railroad ran at ground level at that time, so electricity was shut off on the third rail until the bank was fully moved on to Front Street. Ironically, Bill Colfer, in charge of the highway department at the time and former historical society president, was responsible for the move. Fearing the worst, he was greeted warmly when he came to work the next morning. The story was carried by a news service and appeared in a Honolulu, Hawaii newspaper, which praised the move as an example of what a bank would do for its customers! This is a fine example of the axiom that's there's no such thing as bad publicity.

Several generations of the Meyer family lived in the Massapequas and owned a farm in the Farm District. John, who was the historical society's public relations representative, was born in 1933 and traced his family back to 1866, when his ancestors came from Hanover. His family owned a farm just north of Jerusalem Avenue. He wrote affectionately about living on the farm and engaging in the usual farming activities with other friends who lived on adjacent farms. He remembered going to the Korean War in 1950 and returning in 1953, amazed at the changes. In those few years, several farms were sold off and many private houses were built throughout the Massapequas. He had learned carpentry by working with his father, so he became very busy working for several builders throughout the area, replacing his friends' farms with new houses.

One of the best-known institutions in the Massapequas is All-American Burgers, located at the southeast corner of Merrick Road and Division Avenue. The business was begun by Philip Vultaggio, who was also responsible for building houses in the area and later in Delray Beach,

Florida. His family later bought the franchise of the Carvel Ice Cream store just west of All American. The Carvel franchise was purchased outright by the Vultaggios in 2000 and renamed Marshall's. Both stores are popular and are crowded every afternoon and evening.

All American and Marshall's are built on the site of the fifth hole of the golf course designed and operated by the Massapequa Hotel. The eighteen-hole course extended from Ocean Avenue to Hicksville Road and Merrick Road down to about Clinton Place today. The course remained popular after Joseph Snedeker sold the hotel in 1914, and it remained open until after World War II, when it was replaced by private houses.

A visit to Woodloch Pines was a rite of passage for many Massapequans. The resort was opened in 1958 by Harry Kiesendahl, who owned a candy store on Broadway, and Don Kranich, who owned the Massapequa Sunoco Station on Park Boulevard. They purchased a resort near Teedyusking Lake in the eastern Poconos. Harry's wife, Mary, had visited the area as a young girl and thought highly of it. The partners opened several lodges and promoted the Pines as an inclusive family resort, offering up to three meals daily and activities for all family members. Many Massapequans visited there in the next several decades, and it still attracts locals. It is still owned by the Kiesendahl family.

Longtime residents remember swimming from the beach at the end of Alhambra Avenue and taking swimming lessons from the American Red Cross. The beach was just south of the Tides on the Bay Restaurant and about one hundred yards from Dick and Dora's, a neighborhood restaurant opened in 1931. Both have disappeared. The only public beach in the Massapequas is Florence Avenue Beach (also known as Philip Healey Beach), at the extreme southwest of the area.

An event shocked the entire community at Massapequa High School in the spring of 1958 when one student murdered another. Bruce Zator and Timothy Wall had argued over a girl several days previously. Zator was suspended but entered the school on April 30 and shot Wall in a boys' bathroom. One historical society trustee's brother witnessed the shooting. Zator was captured, pleaded guilty to manslaughter and was sentenced to ten to twenty years in prison at Elmira Correctional Facility. He died of cancer while in prison.

The name Massapequa is attached to two U.S. Navy ships. The first SS *Massapequa* was a cargo ship, built in 1893 and used to carry goods across the Atlantic Ocean. It was torpedoed and sunk by a German submarine on July 7, 1917, while transporting food and clothing for the Belgian war effort. The entire crew was able to reach a small island off the Belgian coast and was rescued. The other ship was a tugboat, launched in 1970 and designed for large harbors. It was based in Yokosuka, Japan, and was active until 2011.

Several famous people lived in the Massapequas at various times. Best known may be the Baldwin brothers (Alec, Daniel, Stephen and William), whose father was physical education director at the high school. For a summer, they lived in the servants' cottage now located at the Historic Complex while their home was repaired after a fire. Brian Setzer also lived here, as did Neil Diamond; radio personality John Gambling; Jerry Seinfeld, whose father owned a sign company; NFL linemen Brian, Gary and Rick Baldinger; James Dolan, owner of the New York Knicks; Carlo Gambino; ballet dancer Andre Eglevsky, who owned a dance studio on Merrick Road; actor Matt Bennett; and Joey Buttafuoco.

CONCLUSION

THE MASSAPEQUAS IN 2001

Settling and Shrinking

The rush of home buyers to the Massapequas after the war slowed down in the 1980s, simply because there was very little room available to build houses. Many who had settled in the 1945–60 period moved away, often to southern states such as Florida or Arizona, for cheaper living conditions and warmer weather. Their relocations led to a shrinking of Massapequa's numbers. The student body throughout the public school system dropped from 15,564 in 1968 to 10,566 in 1980 and to 7,000 in 1993, about where it stands today. The faculty count declined from 807 in 1970 to 681 in 1980.

Herbert Pluschau was the superintendent during the '80s, having served as a physical education teacher and guidance counselor, among other roles. He was a charismatic leader and characterized as a "doer"; he drew on his good relations with the faculty, union and community to reshape the system. Ames School closed in 1987, and Hawthorn was converted into a community center and later a police training academy. Berner was converted from a high school to a junior high that same year, ending a bitter rivalry between the two high schools and confirming the decline of the district's population.

Grace Church membership declined from 2,310 in 1968 to 1,251 in 1992 and 696 in 2000. As noted earlier, the Jewish population of Nassau

County declined significantly as well. The town of Oyster Bay's population reflected the trend:

- 1940: 42,594
- 1950: 66,930
- 1960: 290,055
- 1970: 333,342
- 1985: 305,730
- 2018: 298,388

Massapequa Park reached its population peak in 1970, with 22,112 residents. It declined to 18,044 by 1990 and stood at 17,163 in 2019. These declines would appear to be the result of the aging of "baby boomers," those born between 1945 and 1964, who filled the schools in the '50s and '60s but then matured and either had fewer children than their parents or moved to other areas, typically the southern states, as did their parents, the original settlers. New residents have typically bought existing houses because there is very little space to add to the housing stock. They, as well as existing homeowners, have often expanded their homes to provide more living space for their families. The population decline has brought stability to the Massapequas and allowed leaders to repurpose several features of the area. The enormous changes in the second half of the twentieth century had gradually ebbed to a slow and steady development by the beginning of the twenty-first century.

NOTES

Chapter 1

1. Strong, *Algonquian Peoples of Long Island*, 233–35.
2. Dayan, *Whaling on Long Island*, 10, 23–25.
3. Strong, *Algonquian Peoples of Long Island*, 264.
4. Flushing Remonstrance, New York State Archives.
5. Townsend history is documented and maintained by the Townsend Society, a family group that manages a research and meeting facility in Oyster Bay. Several descendants are diligent in maintaining original records, performing genealogical research, participating in biographical and family society organizations and writing articles about the family's history. An 1865 volume titled "A Memorial of John, Henry, and Richard Townsend" by James C. Townsend details the family's early genealogy. John Townsend is buried at a small cemetery nestled among several private houses in Oyster Bay. Despite the society's efforts, the grave sites of Henry and Thomas have never been discovered.
6. Strong, *Algonquian Peoples of Long Island*, 270.

Chapter 2

7. A letter of marque was a document provided by a king or other public official that allowed a pirate to prey on enemy ships as long as he or

she sent a portion of the spoils to the royal court or public office. See Merchant, *Pirates of Colonial Newport*, 40–41.

8. Jones, *Jones Family of Long Island*, 48.

9. Ibid., 55. There are no portraits or sketches of Thomas Jones or of Freelove. The earliest images of the Joneses are those of Thomas's grandson Judge Thomas Jones and his wife, Anne Delancey Jones.

10. No evidence of William Jones's house has survived, but it appears likely that the West Neck (Jones) Cemetery was built in the back of his property, south of South Country (later Merrick) Road.

Chapter 3

11. Jones, *Jones Family of Long Island*, 82–84.

12. Floyd-Jones, *Thomas Jones, Fort Nesk* [*sic*], 25.

13. Jones, *Jones Family of Long Island*, 90.

14. Ibid.

15. "Act of Attainder," Greenleaf's Laws of New York. The Act of Attainder is considered by historians an extraordinary example of legislative overreach. Such provisions were forbidden by Article I of the U.S. Constitution.

16. Jones, *Jones Family of Long Island*, 122, 155.

17. Hughes, *Cold Spring Harbor*, 77, 91.

18. Noble, *Legacy*.

19. Spinzia, "Women of Long Island," 3–7.

20. *New York Times*, "Mary Gardiner Jones."

21. Floyd-Jones, *Thomas Jones, Fort Nesk* [*sic*], 182.

Chapter 4

22. The area was known as South Oyster Bay until the late 1800s. Queens Land and Title Company began to call it Massapequa about 1890, and the new train station, built with money provided by George Stanton Floyd-Jones in 1890, was named Massapequa.

23. The information about Massapequa Manor is taken from files provided to the historical society of the Massapequas in 2016 by Jack Corroon, who was born in the house in 1922.

24. Massapequa Water District customers typically receive water bills that appear to be much less than New York American Water's customers, but the difference is made up by a water tax imposed by the Town of Oyster Bay. Information provided by Constance Belagrinos, business manager of the Massapequa Water District.
25. Wiley, *Preacher's Son*, 28.
26. Ibid., 27–28. Efforts by the historical society to find the trough and cup were fruitless, but the sign stands as a reminder of the huge differences in the area between today and slightly more than one hundred years ago.
27. "Little Unqua."
28. Goodenough, "Baldwin-Hilbert House," 1.
29. Kirchmann, "When 'Old Grace' Was New," 16–18.
30. Delancey Floyd-Jones Papers, Commendation.

Chapter 5

31. See Meyer, *Massapequa's Farm District* and *Growing Up Big in a Small Town*.
32. "390 Ocean Avenue."
33. Belagrinos, Massapequa Water District files.
34. The Long Island Railroad was extended to New York City in 1910, when a tunnel was constructed under the East River and track laid to Penn Station.
35. Seyfried, *Long Island Rail Road*, 1:57.

Chapter 6

36. Kirchmann, "Massapequa School."
37. *Small Houses of the Twenties*.
38. Hotson, *The Bremen*, passim.
39. Bayor and Meagher, *New York Irish*, 410–12.
40. Ibid.

Chapter 7

41. Much of the material in this section is covered in greater detail in George Kirchmann's *From Mansions to Suburbia* (Author House, 2019).

42. Chart of house prices derived from several real estate pamphlets in the files of the Historical Society of the Massapequas.
43. Belagrinos, Massapequa Water District files.
44. Pluschau, "Story about the Massapequa Schools."
45. Figures supplied by School District 23.
46. Pluschau, "Story about the Massapequa Schools," passim.
47. Moran, "Massapequa Public Library," 6.
48. *50 Years of Memories*, n.p.
49. Annunziato, "History of St. David's Lutheran Church."
50. "Massapequa Reformed Church: Our History."
51. Leonard, *Richly Blessed*, 73–91; "History of St. Rose of Lima Parish."
52. Kreisel, "From Orchard Street to Sunrise Highway," 190–91.
53. Andersen, Long Island Rail Road History.

Chapter 8

54. Cramer, "$10 Saves Church from Ruin." Much of the information regarding Old Grace Church is the result of conversations with Lillian Bryson and Arlene Goodenough, who were involved in the process from the beginning. Both women were longtime active members of Grace Church, as well as historical society members from the late '70s.
55. *Newsletter of the Historical Society of the Massapequas*, notice, 3.
56. The original marker was stolen and never recovered. A new marker was erected in 1998.

BIBLIOGRAPHY

This list includes books that were not cited in the notes but that provided useful information.

"Act of Attainder." Greenleaf's Laws of New York, Chapter XXIII, October 22, 1779.

Andersen, Bob. Long Island Rail Road History. http://lirrhistory.com.

Annunziato, Ruth. "The History of St. David's Lutheran Church in Massapequa Park, New York." Unpublished, 2001.

Bayor, Raymond, and Timothy Meagher. *The New York Irish*. Baltimore, MD: Johns Hopkins University Press, 1996.

Bleyer, Bill. *Long Island and the Sea*. Charleston, SC: The History Press, 2019.

Cramer, Paul. "$10 Saves Church from Ruin." Local newspaper, source unknown, n.d.

Dayan, Nomi. *Whaling on Long Island*. Charleston, SC: Arcadia Publishing, 2016.

Delancey Floyd-Jones Papers. Commendation. Special Collections, University of Texas at Arlington Library.

Dolan, Eric. *Leviathan: The History of Whaling in America*. New York: W.W. Norton, 2007.

Doyle, Irving. *The History of Old Harbour Green, 1931 to 1983*. N.p.: printed privately, n.d.

Dugard, Martin. *The Training Ground*. New York: Little Brown and Company, 2008.

Eberlein, Harold D. *Manor Houses and Historic Homes of Long Island and Staten Island.* Port Washington, NY: Ira J. Friedman Inc., 1928.

50 Years of Memories: Celebration Weekend, May 3, 1997. Anniversary Booklet of Community United Methodist Church.

Floyd-Jones, Delancey. *Letters from the Far East.* New York: Public Service Publishing Company, 1887.

Floyd-Jones, Thomas. *Backward Glances: Reminiscences of an Old New Yorker.* New York, 1914.

———. *Thomas Jones, Fort Nesk [sic], Queens County Long Island, 1695 and His Descendants the Floyd-Jones Family, with Connections from the Year 1066.* New York: J. Grant Senia Press, 1906.

Flushing Remonstrance. New York State Archives. NYSA_1809_78_Vo8_0689.

Freeman, Paul. Abandoned and Little-Known Airfields: New York. https://www.airfields-freeman.com/ny.

Goodenough, Arlene. "The Baldwin-Hilbert House." *The Freeholder* 1, no. 1 (Summer 1996): 1.

———. "South Oyster Bay Militia Called Up for New York's Defense." *The Freeholder* 2, no. 3 (Winter 1998): 7–8.

———. "The Van De Water Hotel of Massapequa." *The Freeholder* 1, no. 2 (Fall 1996): 2.

———. "A Visit to Massapequa in 435 B.C." *The Freeholder* 4, no. 3 (Winter 2000): 20–21.

"History of St. Rose of Lima Parish." N.p., 2010.

Hotson, Fred. *The Bremen.* Toronto, CA: Canav Books, 1988.

Hughes, Robert. *Cold Spring Harbor.* Charleston, SC: Arcadia Publishing, 2014.

Jones, John H. *The Jones Family of Long Island: Descendants of Major Thomas Jones (1665–1713) and Allied Families.* New York: Tobias A. Wright, 1907.

Jones, Mary Gardiner. *Tearing Down Walls: A Woman's Triumph.* Lanham, MD: Hamilton Books, 2008.

Jones, Thomas. *History of New York during the Revolutionary War.* New York: Trow's Printing and Bookbinding, 1879.

Kirchmann, George. "Massapequa School." *Signs of the Times. Massapequa's Historical Markers.* Massapequa, NY: George Kirchmann, 2017.

———. "When 'Old Grace' Was New." *The Freeholder* 3, no. 4 (Spring 1999): 16–18.

Klein, Rich, and Lisa Glass. *Massapequa: A Pictorial History through the Eyes of Baby Boomers.* Np, 2014.

Kreisel, Martha. "From Orchard Street to Sunrise Highway." In *Nassau County: From Rural Hinterland to Suburban Metropolis*. Edited by Joanne P. Krieg and Natalie A. Naylor. Interlaken, NY: Head of the Lakes Publishing, 2000.

Krieg, Joann, and Natalie Naylor, eds. *To Know the Place: Exploring Long Island History*. Interlaken, NY: Head of the Lakes Publishing, 1995.

Leonard, Joan de Lourdes, Sr. *Richly Blessed: The Diocese of Rockville Center, 1957–1990*. Marceline, MO: Walsworth Publishing Company, 1991.

Lipman, Andrew. *The Saltwater Frontier: Indians and the Contest for the American Coast*. New Haven, CT: Yale University Press, 2015.

"Little Unqua." File available at the Historical Society of the Massapequas.

The Long Island Almanac. Ronkonkoma, NY: Long Island Business, 1997.

Long Island Regional Planning Board. *Historical Population of Long Island Communities, 1789–1980*.

Marshall, Bernice. *Colonial Hempstead: Long Island Life under the Dutch and English*. New York: J. Friedman, 1962.

"Massapequa Reformed Church: Our History." Unpublished, 2012.

Merchant, Gloria. *Pirates of Colonial Newport*. Charleston, SC: The History Press, 2014.

Meyer, John H. *Growing Up Big in a Small Town*. N.p.: printed privately, n.d.

———. *Massapequa's Farm District, 1800s–1950s*. N.p.: printed privately, n.d.

Miller, Rhoda. *The Jewish Community of Long Island*. Charleston, SC: Arcadia Publishing, 2016.

Moran, Virginia. "Massapequa Public Library." *Massapequa's Annual* (Fall 1956): 6.

Naylor, Natalie. "General Rosalie Jones (1883–1978): Oyster Bay's Maverick Suffragette." *The Freeholder* 12, no. 1 (Summer 2007): 3–7, 19.

Newman-Brooks, Lorraine. *Massapequa: From the Time of the Native Americans to the Year 2000*. New York, n.d.

Newsletter of the Historical Society of the Massapequas. Notice (Summer 1988): 3.

New York Times. "Mary Gardiner Jones, Consumer Advocate, Dies at 89." January 7, 2010, 25.

Noble, Dr. Dennis L. *A Legacy: The United States Life-Saving Service*. N.p.: printed privately, n.d.

Norton, Marybeth. *The British Americans. The Loyalist Exiles in England, 1774–1789*. New York: Little Brown, 1972.

Onderdonck, Henry. *Queens County in Olden Times*. N.p., 1865.

"Our Lady of Lourdes Parish History." Online history provided by the parish, 2013.

Pluschau, Herbert. "A Story about the Massapequa Schools." Unedited draft, 2008. Available through the Massapequa School District.

Prichard, Robert W. *A History of the Episcopal Church*. New York: Morehouse Publishing, 2014.

Seyfried, Vincent. *The Long Island Rail Road. A Comprehensive History*. Vol. 1. Garden City, New York: self-published, 1961.

Small Houses of the Twenties: The Sears, Roebuck 1926 House Catalog. New York: Dover Publications, 1991.

Solecki, Ralph S., and Robert S. Grumet. "The Fort Massapeag Archaeological Site National Historic Landmark." *The Bulletin: Journal of the New York State Archaeological Association* 108 (Fall 1994): 18–27.

Spinzia, Judith Ader. "Women of Long Island: Mary Elizabeth Jones, Rosalie Gardiner Jones." *The Freeholder* 11 (Spring 2007): 3–7.

Stone, Gaynell, ed. *Native Forts of the Long Island Sound Area*. Stony Brook, NY: Suffolk County Archaeological Association, 2006.

Strong, John. *The Algonquian Peoples of Long Island from Earliest Times to 1700*. Interlaken, NY: Heart of the Lakes Publishing, 1997.

The Temple Judea Story. Provided by the Temple, 2008.

"390 Ocean Avenue." Statement of Significance Summary Paragraph, U.S. Department of the Interior, OMB No. 1024-0018.

Townsend, James C. *A Memorial of John, Henry, and Richard Townsend and Their Descendants*. New York: W.A. Townsend Publisher, 1865.

Wiley, Ralph Houghton. *Preacher's Son. Parish Baby—Yacht Builder—Sailor*. New York: Vantage Press, 1972.

INDEX

ABOUT THE AUTHOR

G eorge Kirchmann is a historian and writer based in Massapequa Park,
New York. A trustee with the Historical Society of the Massapequas,
he writes for its regular newsletter and for several local publications. He is a
member of the Nassau County Historical Society and the Seaford Historical
Society. George holds a BA in history from the Catholic University of
America and a PhD in history from the City University of New York.

Visit us at
www.historypress.com

www.ingramcontent.com/pod-product-compliance
Lightning Source LLC
Chambersburg PA
CBHW070925150426
42812CB00049B/1489